# EFFICIENT ASSET MANAGEMENT

# Financial Management Association Survey and Synthesis Series

*The Search for Value: Measuring the Company's Cost of Capital*
  Michael C. Ehrhardt

*Lease or Buy? Principles for Sound Decision Making*
  James S. Schallheim

*Derivatives: A Comprehensive Resource for Options, Futures, Interest Rate Swaps, and Mortgage Securities*
  Fred D. Arditti

*Managing Pension Plans: A Comprehensive Guide to Improving Plan Performance*
  Dennis E. Logue and Jack S. Rader

*Efficient Asset Management: A Practical Guide to Stock Portfolio Optimization and Asset Allocation*
  Richard O. Michaud

# EFFICIENT ASSET MANAGEMENT

## A Practical Guide to Stock Portfolio Optimization and Asset Allocation

Richard O. Michaud

Harvard Business School Press
Boston, Massachusetts

02 01 00 99 98   5 4 3 2 1

**Library of Congress Cataloging-in-Publication Data**
Michaud, Richard O., 1941–
    Efficient asset management: a practical guide to stock
portfolio optimization and asset allocation / Richard O. Michaud.
       p.   cm. — (Financial Management Association survey and
synthesis series)
    Includes index.
    ISBN 0-87584-743-9 (alk. paper)
    1. Investment analysis—Mathematical models.  2. Portfolio
management—Mathematical models.  I. Title.  II. Series.
HG4529.M53   1998
332.6—dc21                             98-5193
                                       CIP

Text design by Wilson Graphics & Design (Kenneth J. Wilson)

*To*

*My Mother, Helena Talbot Michaud*

*My Father, Omer Michaud, and his cherished memory*

*Robin Esch, a wise, unerring mentor*

# Contents

*Preface*  xiii

*Chapter 1:* **Introduction**  1

Markowitz Efficiency  1

An Asset Management Tool  2

Traditional Objections  3

The Most Important Limitations  3

Resolving the Limitations of Mean-Variance Optimization  4

Illustrating the Techniques  5

*Chapter 2:* **Classic Mean-Variance Optimization**  7

Portfolio Risk and Return  7

Defining Markowitz Efficiency  9

Optimization Constraints  9

The Residual Risk-Return Efficient Frontier  10

Computational Algorithms  10

Asset Allocation versus Equity Portfolio Optimization  11

A Global Asset Allocation Example  13

Reference Portfolios and Portfolio Analysis  16

Return Premium Efficient Frontiers  16

**Appendix: Mathematical Formulation of Mean-Variance
Efficiency**  20

*Chapter 3:* **Traditional Criticisms and Alternatives**  23

Alternative Measures of Risk  23

Utility Function Optimization  25

Multiperiod Investment Horizons  26

Asset-Liability Financial Planning Studies  29

Linear Programming Optimization  31

*Chapter 4:*  **Understanding Mean-Variance Efficiency**  33

The Fundamental Limitations of Mean-Variance Efficiency  33

Repeating Jobson and Korkie  35

Implications of Jobson and Korkie Analysis  36

The Statistical Character of Mean-Variance Efficiency  36

Efficient Frontier Variance  36

The Statistical Equivalence Region  37

A Practical Investment Tool?  39

*Chapter 5:*  **Portfolio Review and Mean-Variance Efficiency**  41

Portfolio Review and Statistical Inference  41

Tests of Asset Pricing Models  41

Heuristic Inference  42

A Sample Acceptance Region  42

Statistical Inference for a Target Efficient Portfolio  45

Rank-Associated Efficient Portfolios  45

*Chapter 6:*  **Portfolio Analysis and the Resampled Efficient Frontier**  49

Conceptual Portfolio Statistical Analysis  49

Efficient Portfolio Statistical Analysis  49

The Resampled Efficient Frontier  55

True and Estimated Optimization Inputs  56

Testing Resampled Efficiency  56

Properties of Resampled Efficient Frontiers  60

Resampled Efficient Frontier Range  61

Caveats  61

Conclusion  62

**Appendix: Resampled Efficiency Tests and Alternatives**  63

*Chapter 7:*  **Portfolio Revision and Confidence Regions**  71

Confidence Intervals and Regions  71

Resampled Efficiency and Distance Functions  72

Resampled Efficient Frontier Confidence Regions  73

Simultaneous Confidence Intervals  75

Examples of Simultaneous Confidence Intervals  76

Ambiguity and Portfolio Efficiency  77

Practical Considerations  79

**Appendix A: Confidence Region for the Sample Mean Vector**  80

**Appendix B: Computing Confidence Regions and Simultaneous Intervals**  81

*Chapter 8:*  **Input Estimation and Stein Estimators**  83

Admissible Estimators  84

Bayesian Procedures and Priors  84

Four Stein Estimators  85

James-Stein Estimator  85

James-Stein Mean-Variance Efficiency  86

James-Stein Estimator Test of Resampled and Mean-Variance Efficiency  90

Frost-Savarino Estimator  93

Covariance Estimation  94

Stein Covariance Estimation  96

Forecasting Stock Risk and Return  97

Utility Functions and Input Estimation  97

Ad Hoc Estimators  98

Conclusions  98

**Appendix: Ledoit Covariance Estimation**  99

*Chapter 9:*  **Benchmark Active Asset Allocation**  101

Benchmark-Relative Active Asset Allocation  102

Implied-Return Asset Allocation   105

Comparing Implied-Return and Benchmark-Relative Frontiers   109

Scaling and Implied Returns   109

Roll's Analysis   112

Additional Procedures   113

*Chapter 10:*  **Investment Policy and Economic Liabilities**   115

Misusing Mean-Variance Efficiency   115

Economic Liability Models   116

An Example: Endowment Fund Investment Policy   117

Pension Liabilities and Benchmark Optimization   117

Limitations of Actuarial Liability Estimation   118

Economic Significance of Variable Liabilities   120

Economic Characteristics of Variable Liabilities   121

An Example: Economic Liability Pension Investment Policy   122

Conclusion   126

*Chapter 11:*  **Return Forecasts and Mixed Estimation**   127

Asset Allocation and Ad Hoc Inputs   127

Mixed Estimation Forecasts   128

Mixed Estimation Asset Allocation Inputs   128

Index-Relative Active Asset Allocation   128

Benefits   130

Equity Return Forecasts and Mixed Estimation   130

*Chapter 12:*  **Avoiding Optimization Errors**   133

Scaling Inputs   133

Financial Reality   135

Liquidity Factors   135

Constraints   135

Biased Portfolio Characteristics  136

Index Funds and Optimizers  137

Optimization from Cash  138

Forecast Return Limitations  139

Conclusion  140

*Epilogue*  141

*Bibliography*  143

*Index*  149

# Preface

*E*ffective asset management is not simply a matter of finding attractive investments. It also requires optimally structuring the portfolio of the assets. This is because the investment behavior of a portfolio is typically different from that of the assets in it. For example, the risk of a portfolio of U.S. equities is often only half that of the average risk of the stocks in it.

Most institutional investors and financial economists acknowledge the investment benefits of efficient portfolio diversification. Optimally managing portfolio risk is an essential component of modern asset management. Markowitz (1959, 1987) has given the classic definition of portfolio optimality. A portfolio is efficient if it has the highest expected (mean) return for a given level of risk (variance) or, equivalently, least risk for a given level of expected return, of all portfolios from a given universe of securities. Markowitz mean-variance (MV) efficiency is a convenient framework for defining portfolio optimality and for constructing optimal stock portfolios and asset allocations. A number of commercial services provide optimizers for computing MV efficient portfolios.

## Investor Acceptance

Modern asset management typically employs many financial theoretical concepts and advanced analytic techniques. Perhaps the most outstanding example is in the management of derivative instruments. Within 15 years of the publication of seminal papers (Black and Scholes 1973, Merton 1973) and the opening of derivative exchanges, an extensive industry applying quantitative techniques to derivative strategies has emerged. In similar fashion, many fixed income managers use sophisticated portfolio structuring techniques for cash flow liability management.[1] In contrast, many institutional managers do not use MV optimizers to structure equity portfolios or define optimal asset allocations.

The relatively low level of analytic sophistication in the culture of institutional equity management is one often-cited reason for the lack of acceptance of MV optimization. There are also organizational and political issues. The investment policy committee and an optimizer perform essentially the same integrative investment func-

---

[1] Leibowitz (1986) describes some of these techniques.

tion. Consequently, the firm's senior investment officers may view an optimizer, and the quantitative specialist who manages it, as usurping their roles and challenging their control and political power in the organization.

It is hard to imagine, however, why investment managers do not behave in their own, as well as their clients', best interests. Experience in derivatives and fixed income management indicates that the investment community quickly adopts highly sophisticated analytics and computer technology when useful. If cultural, political, or competence factors limit the use of MV optimizers in traditional investment organizations, new firms are likely to form without these limitations, with the objective of leveraging the technology and dominating the industry. Indeed many "quantitative" equity management firms, formed over the last 25 years, have this objective. However, the "Markowitz optimization enigma"—the fact that many equity managers ignore MV optimization—can be largely explained without recourse to irrationality, incompetence, or politics (Michaud 1989a). The basic problem is that MV portfolio efficiency has fundamental investment limitations as a practical tool of asset management. It is likely that the limitations of MV optimizers have been an important factor in limiting the success of many quantitative equity managers over the last 25 years.

### The Fundamental Issue

Although Markowitz efficiency is a convenient and useful theoretical framework for defining portfolio optimality, in practice it is an error-prone procedure that often results in "error-maximized" and "investment-irrelevant" portfolios (Jobson and Korkie 1980, 1981, Michaud 1989a). Proposed alternatives share similar, if not even more significant, limitations. The limitations of MV efficiency in practice generally derive from a lack of statistical understanding of MV optimization. A "statistical" view of MV optimization leads to new procedures that can reduce or eliminate many of its most serious deficiencies. A statistical view also alters the perception of portfolio efficiency and challenges the value of some popular investment practices and academic research.

### Overview

This book describes the problems of MV optimization as a practical tool of institutional asset management. It reviews various proposed alternatives to MV optimization and describes their limitations. A "statistical" perspective of MV efficiency serves as a route for developing powerful techniques to enhance the practical value of optimized portfolios. In particular, new tools for portfolio analysis help to reduce instability and ambiguity. In addition, various institutional tools for implementing optimizations can help to avoid errors.

The goal is to define an optimization process that validly reflects investment insights while maintaining the rigor, informational breadth, and convenience that MV optimization provides. A simple asset allocation illustrates the issues and new procedures. The text maintains a practical perspective throughout.

The book's proposals for managing portfolios and enhancing asset management include the following:

- *The "Resampled Efficient Frontier":* A new criterion for defining portfolio optimality that may often enhance investment value.

- *Improved Estimators:* Input estimation methods that reduce statistical noise and optimization ambiguity.

- *Inference:* Tests for portfolio efficiency that may avoid unnecessary portfolio revisions and reduce trading costs.

- *Portfolio Analysis:* Rules for revising portfolios that reduce the need for optimization.

- *Benchmark Optimization:* The introduction of portfolio priors that redefine the optimization framework and reduce optimization ambiguity.

- *Mixed Estimation:* A method for rigorously including exogenous return forecasts with historical data that reduces optimization instability.

- *Institutional Techniques:* A list of specialized techniques and practices to manage the optimization process and avoid errors.

### Features and Scope

This text is the first to integrate and systematically treat MV optimization from a statistical, rather than a computational technique, point of view. The focus is to enhance the investment value of portfolio construction techniques in practice.

The academic literature on MV optimization often allows short selling. In contrast, most institutional equity portfolios and asset allocations are sign constrained.[2] Optimization without short selling is more analytically difficult and often leads to qualitatively different results. Except as noted, short selling is not assumed.

The scope of the book is limited to managing stock portfolios and asset allocations. These areas include many asset management situations of practical investment interest. A discussion of the benefits and limitations of popular alternatives to MV optimization is included.

### Audience and Analytic Requirements

Knowledge of statistical methods and modern finance at the level of a relatively nontechnical paper in the *Financial Analysts Journal* or *Journal of Portfolio Management* is desirable. The discussions are mostly self-contained and generally require little additional reading. The technical level required of the reader in the body of the text is relatively minimal. The footnotes and appendices discuss technical issues and topics of special interest.

The primary audience for the text is that of institutional investment practitioners, sophisticated investors, and academic and professional researchers in applied financial economics. Investors, investment managers, consultants, trustees, and brokers will be interested, given the widespread use of MV portfolio construction and asset management techniques and the need to stay current in investment technology. Academic and professional financial economists will have interest when using MV optimization as a research tool. The book may also be useful as a supplement in advanced undergraduate and graduate courses in investment management, in graduate courses in quantitative asset management, and for a course on portfolio optimization in institutional asset management.

### Technical Note

The MATLAB® language (The MathWorks, Inc., Natick, MA, U.S.A.) was used to develop the computational algorithms in the text. Specific MATLAB programs include *qp.m* and *mvnrnd.m*.

### Acknowledgments

I am indebted and most influenced by the pioneering work of J.D. "Dave" Jobson and Bob Korkie on the statistical nature of MV efficiency.

---

[2] This does not rule out consideration of such strategies as long and short market–neutral equity portfolios. In the usual definition of this strategy, each portfolio before shorting has nonnegative portfolio weights (Michaud 1993). The selling short of financial or commodity assets via derivative securities, however, is quite common.

My long-term intellectual debt is to Harry Markowitz, whose work remains seminal in modern finance and investment management. I have benefited from many valuable discussions with Philippe Jorion and Olivier Ledoit. Chapter 12 has benefited from a number of conversations with Paul Erlich. I am indebted to James L. Farrell, Jr., who initially spurred my interest in the topic, and its importance, many years ago; to J. Peter Williamson, who was instrumental in encouraging early development of the manuscript; to Philip Cooley for encouragement and support; and to Barbara Roth for patient and helpful guidance through the stress of the production process. I am also indebted to my colleagues at Acadian Asset Management in Boston, particularly Gary Bergstrom, for forbearance and understanding during the writing of this book. My greatest personal debt remains to my son, Robert. In particular, the key ideas in Chapter 6, including the resampled efficient frontier, is joint work. In addition, he has provided numerous critical insights and occasional corrections during the writing of the manuscript, and he is a primary contributor to the development of the computer algorithms. I am responsible for all remaining errors.

I am pleased to hear from readers. Please send your comments, questions, and corrections to my e-mail address, rmichaud@worldnet.att.net, or visit my Web site at www.rmichaud.com for updates on the book and on research in optimization and investment technology.

# *E*FFICIENT
# *A*SSET
# *M*ANAGEMENT

*Chapter* **1**

# Introduction

## Markowitz Efficiency

Markowitz (1959) mean-variance (MV) efficiency is the classic paradigm of modern finance for efficiently allocating capital among risky assets. Given estimates of expected return, standard deviation or variance, and correlation of return for a set of assets, MV efficiency provides the investor with an exact prescription for optimal allocation of capital. The Markowitz efficient frontier (Exhibit 1.1) represents all efficient portfolios in the sense that all other portfolios have less expected return for a given level of risk or, equivalently, more risk for a given level of expected return. In this framework, the variance or standard deviation of return defines portfolio risk. MV efficiency considers not only the risk and return of securities but also their interrelationships.

Exhibit 1.1 illustrates these concepts: Portfolio A is the investor's current portfolio, with a given expected return and standard deviation. Portfolio B is the efficient portfolio that has less risk at the same level of expected return of portfolio A. Portfolio C is the efficient portfolio that has more expected return at the same level of risk as portfolio A. The efficient frontier describes the mean and standard deviation of all efficient portfolios.

In most modern finance textbooks, MV efficiency is the criterion of choice for defining optimal portfolio structure and for rationalizing the value of diversification. Markowitz efficiency is also the basis for many important advances in positive financial economics. These include the Sharpe (1964)-Lintner (1965) capital asset pricing model and recognition of the fundamental dichotomy between systematic and diversifiable risk.

Many investment situations may use MV efficiency for wealth allocation. An international equity manager may want to find optimal asset allocations among international equity markets based on market

1

**Exhibit 1.1:** Mean-Variance Portfolio Efficiency

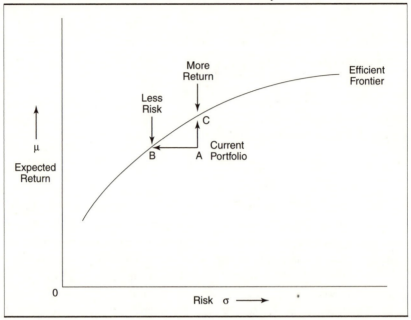

index historic returns. A plan sponsor may want to find an optimal long-term investment policy for allocating assets among domestic and foreign bonds, equities, and other asset classes. A domestic equity manager may want to find the optimal equity portfolio based on forecasts of return and estimated risk. MV optimization is flexible enough to consider various trading costs, institutional and client constraints, and desired levels of risk. In these and other cases, MV efficiency serves as the standard optimization framework for modern asset management.

## An Asset Management Tool

MV optimization is useful as an asset management tool for many applications, including these:

1. Implementing investment objectives and constraints.

2. Controlling the components of portfolio risk.

3. Implementing the asset manager's investment philosophy, style, and market outlook.

4. Efficiently using active return information (Sharpe 1985, 666–70).

5. Conveniently and efficiently imbedding new information into portfolios.

## Traditional Objections

Academics and practitioners have raised a number of objections to MV efficiency as the appropriate framework for defining portfolio optimality. These "traditional" criticisms of MV efficiency tend to fall into one of the following categories:

1. *Investor utility:* The limitations of representing investor utility and investment objectives with the mean and variance of return.

2. *Multiperiod framework:* The limitations of MV efficiency as a single-period framework for investors with long-term investment objectives, such as pension plans and endowment funds.

3. *Asset-liability financial planning:* Claims that asset-liability simulation is a superior approach for asset allocation.

Chapter 3 examines each category of objection in detail. These traditional objections often do not address the most serious limitations of MV optimizers, nor do they provide useful alternatives in many cases. On the other hand, the robustness of MV optimization is often unappreciated, and several workarounds make the MV framework useful in many situations of practical interest.

## The Most Important Limitations

In practice, the most important limitations of MV optimization are instability and ambiguity. MV optimizers function as a chaotic investment decision system. Small changes in input assumptions often imply large changes in the optimized portfolio. Consequently, portfolio optimality is often not well defined. The procedure overuses statistically estimated information and magnifies the impact of estimation errors. It is not simply a matter of garbage in, garbage out, but, rather, a molehill of garbage in, a mountain of garbage out. The result is that optimized portfolios are "error maximized" and often have little, if any, reliable investment value. Indeed, an equally weighted portfolio may often be substantially closer to true MV optimality than an optimized portfolio.

The frequent failure of optimized portfolios to meet practical investment objectives has led a number of sophisticated institutional investors to abandon the method for alternative procedures and to rely increasingly on intuition and priors. The limitations of MV optimization algorithms have also contributed heavily to the lack of widespread acceptance of quantitative equity management. The problems of MV optimization are not easily resolved with alternative risk measures, objective functions, or simulation procedures: They are endemic to most optimization procedures.

## Resolving the Limitations of Mean-Variance Optimization

The problems of MV optimization instability and ambiguity are ultimately those of overfitting data. Statistical estimates define an efficient frontier. Because of variability in the input estimates, many portfolios are statistically as efficient as the ones on the efficient frontier. In other words, an appropriate statistical test would not be able to differentiate the efficiency of many portfolios off the efficient frontier from those on it. A computation of all the "statistically equivalent" efficient portfolios[1] reveals the variability and essential statistical character of MV optimization. A statistical perspective helps to resolve many of the most serious practical limitations of MV optimization and is often associated with a significantly reduced need to trade.

Many of the most important methods for reducing the instability and ambiguity of the optimization process and enhancing its investment value are based on statistical procedures that have largely been ignored by the financial community. These techniques come from financial theory, econometrics, and institutional research and practice.

Practitioners may ignore procedures for enhancing MV optimization for a variety of reasons. The enormous prestige and goodwill Markowitz and his work enjoy in the investment community have led many to ignore the obvious practical limitations of the procedure. Many influential consultants, software providers, and asset managers have vested commercial interests in the status quo. For others, practical considerations have hampered implementation. Until recently, some of the statistical techniques have been inconvenient or inaccessible because they required high-speed computers and advanced mathematical or statistical software. Finally, the statistical character of MV optimization requires a fundamental shift in the notion of portfolio

---

[1] Chapter 4 provides an illustration of statistically equivalent efficient portfolios.

optimality, the need to think statistically, and a significant increase in procedural complexity.

## Illustrating the Techniques

Asset allocations are important in their own right and provide a useful framework for analyzing many fundamental problems of optimization. A simple global asset allocation problem illustrates several of these issues and alternative procedures.

The new methods presented here can significantly reduce the impact of estimation errors, enhance the investment meaning of the results, provide an understanding of precision, and stabilize the optimization. In isolation, each procedure can be helpful; together, they may have a substantial impact on enhancing the investment value of optimized portfolios.

*Chapter* **2**

# Classic Mean-Variance Optimization

*T*his chapter describes in relatively simple terms some of the essential technical issues that characterize MV optimization and portfolio efficiency. For the sake of compact discussion, the introduction of some basic assumptions and mathematical notation is useful. An example of an asset allocation optimization illustrates the techniques presented here.

## Portfolio Risk and Return

Suppose estimates of expected returns, variances or standard deviations, and correlations for a universe of assets.[1] The expected return, $\mu$ (mu), of a portfolio of assets $P$, $\mu_p$, is the portfolio-weighted expected return for each asset.[2] The variance $\sigma^2$ (sigma squared) of a portfolio of assets $P$, $\sigma_p^2$, depends on the portfolio weights, the variance of the assets in the portfolio, and the correlation, $\rho$ (rho), between pairs of assets.[3] The standard deviation $\sigma$ is the square root of the variance and is

---

[1] As noted below, the covariance can also define the optimization risk parameters.

[2] Let $\mu_i$, $i = 1 \ldots N$ refer to the expected return for asset $i$ in the $N$ asset universe. Let $w_i$ refer to the weight of asset $i$ in portfolio $P$. The sum of portfolio weights $w_i$ times the expected returns $\mu_i$ for each asset $i$ in the universe is equal to the expected return for portfolio $P$. In mathematical notation, the symbol $\Sigma_i$ denotes the summation from 1 to $N$, and the portfolio expected return is defined as $\mu_p = \Sigma_i w_i {}^* \mu_i$.

[3] The variance of portfolio $P$, $\sigma_p^2$, is the double sum of the product for all ordered pairs of assets of the portfolio weight for asset $i$, the portfolio weight for asset $j$, the standard deviation for asset $i$, the standard deviation for asset $j$, and the correlation between asset $i$ and $j$. In mathematical notation, $\sigma_p^2 = \Sigma_i \Sigma_j w_i {}^* w_j {}^* \sigma_i {}^* \sigma_j {}^* \rho_{i,j}$, where $\sigma$ is the standard deviation (square root of the variance) and $\rho$ is the correlation. The quantity $\sigma_{i,j}$ is known as the covariance. It is equal to $\sigma_i {}^* \sigma_j {}^* \rho_{i,j}$ and is often used as an alternate way to define the variance. The covariance matrix consists of all ordered pairs of the covariances.

a useful alternative for describing asset risk. One reason for preferring the standard deviation to the variance is that it is expressed in the same units of return as the mean.

Exhibit 2.1 shows the mean and standard deviation for a portfolio consisting of two assets. It illustrates some essential properties of portfolio expected return and risk. Asset 1 has an expected return of 5% and risk of 10%, and asset 2 has an expected return of 10% and risk of 20%. Five curves connect the two assets and display the risk and expected return of portfolios, ranging from 100% of capital in asset 1 to 100% in asset 2. The asset correlations associated with the five curves (from right to left) are 1.0, 0.5, 0.0, −0.5, and −1.0.

The five curves illustrate how correlations and portfolio weights affect portfolio risk and expected return. When the correlation is 1, as in the extreme right-hand curve in the exhibit, portfolio risk and expected return is a weighted average of the risk and return of the two assets. In this case, there is no benefit to diversification. In all other cases, except for the assets themselves, portfolio risk is less than the weighted average of the risk of the assets. In most cases, asset correlations are less than 1. United States stock correlations are often within 0.3 to 0.5 range. As the level of correlation diminishes, the amount of

**Exhibit 2.1:** Portfolio Risk and Return: Two-Asset Case

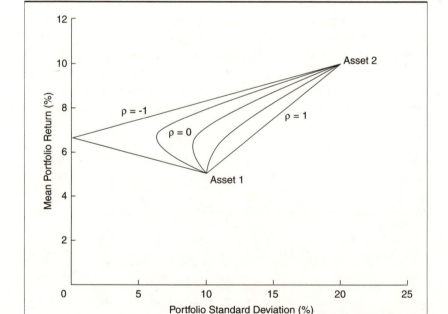

available risk reduction increases. In the case of a −1 correlation between two assets (the extreme left-hand curve), it is possible to eliminate portfolio risk.

## Defining Markowitz Efficiency

Exhibit 2.1 shows that an appropriate set of portfolio weights may significantly reduce portfolio risk in many cases. The notion of defining an optimal set of portfolio weights to optimize risk and return is the basis of Markowitz portfolio efficiency. The efficiency criterion states:

A portfolio $P^*$ is MV efficient if it has least risk for a given level of portfolio expected return.[4]

The MV efficiency criterion is equivalent to maximizing expected portfolio return for a given level of portfolio risk:

A portfolio $P^*$ is MV efficient if it has the maximum expected return for a given level of portfolio risk.[5]

Which formulation of portfolio efficiency is used is a matter of convenience.

As Exhibit 1.1 indicates, each portfolio on the efficient frontier satisfies the efficiency criterion. The efficient frontier is monotone increasing in the mean as a function of increasing portfolio risk.

## Optimization Constraints

Various linear constraints are generally included in an MV optimization. In practice, optimizations typically assume that the portfolio weights sum to 1 (budget constraint)[6] and are nonnegative (no-short-selling constraint).[7] The budget condition is a linear equality constraint on the optimization. The no-short-selling condition is a set of sign constraints, or linear inequalities (one for each asset in the optimization). The budget and no-short-selling conditions form a base case set of optimization constraints. Many institutional portfolios satisfy base case as-

---

[4] Formally, portfolio $P^*$ is MV efficient if, for any portfolio $P$, $\mu_p = \mu_{p*}$ implies that $\sigma_p^2 \geq \sigma_{p*}^2$.

[5] Formally, portfolio $P^*$ is MV efficient if, for any portfolio $P$, $\sigma_p^2 = \sigma_{p*}^2$ implies that $\mu_p \leq \mu_{p*}$.

[6] In mathematical notation, the budget constraint implies that $\Sigma_i w_i = 1$.

[7] In mathematical notation, $w_i \geq 0$ for all portfolio assets.

sumptions. In practice, an optimization often includes additional linear inequality and equality constraints, particularly for equity portfolios. Except as noted, all the optimizations in the text assume budget and sign constraints.

## The Residual Risk-Return Efficient Frontier

An often-used variation of classic Markowitz MV efficiency, which may be called benchmark optimization, is based on "residual" return. (Given an appropriate benchmark, the difference between asset and benchmark return defines residual return.) It is convenient to use the following notation for MV residual return efficiency. Let

$\alpha$  = expected residual return

$\omega^2$ = residual return variance

The definition of Markowitz efficiency for residual return is precisely the same as before, with $\alpha$ and $\omega$ replacing $\mu$ and $\sigma$.

By definition, the benchmark has zero expected residual return and residual risk. In many applications, a portfolio, such as an index, defines the benchmark. Exhibit 2.2 illustrates the notion of MV residual return efficiency. In this case, an investor with portfolio A wants to optimize expected residual return at the same level of residual risk. The exhibit assumes that the benchmark return is a feasible portfolio. The efficient frontier is the collection of all portfolios with maximum $\alpha$ for all possible levels of portfolio residual risk.

## Computational Algorithms

Several methods are available for estimating MV efficient portfolios. The method used may depend on the constraints. For example, an MV optimization that includes only linear equality constraints, such as the budget constraint, can be solved analytically with matrix algebra in a way very similar to a linear regression.[8] On the other hand, an MV optimization that includes linear inequality constraints, such as sign constraints, generally requires numerical analysis procedures for solution.

*Quadratic programming* is the technical term for the numerical analysis procedure used to compute MV efficient portfolios in practice. Quadratic programming algorithms allow maximization of expected

---

[8] See, for example, Alexander and Francis (1986) and Jobson and Korkie (1983).

**Exhibit 2.2:** Residual Risk and Return Mean-Variance Efficiency

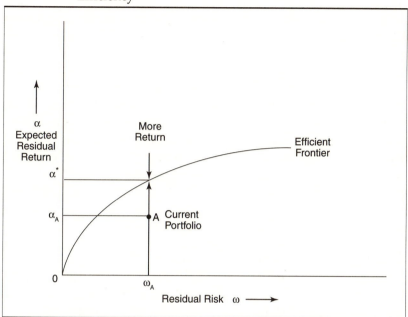

return and minimization of the variance, subject to linear equality and inequality constraints. The term *quadratic* refers to the variance in the optimization objective; *programming* refers to optimizations that include linear inequality as well as equality constraints.

Many algorithms are used for computing MV efficient portfolios. The choice may depend on convenience, computational speed, number of assets, number and character of constraints, and the required accuracy. Various tradeoffs govern the choice of the optimum algorithm for a given problem.[9] In the optimization examples in this and following chapters, the modest number of assets allows for the use of an exact quadratic programming procedure.[10]

## Asset Allocation versus Equity Portfolio Optimization

Asset allocation and equity portfolio optimization are the two most popular applications of MV optimization. In both cases, the optimiza-

---

[9] See the appendix at the end of this chapter.

[10] The procedure uses the simplex algorithm and active set method.

tion finds optimal allocations of capital to maximize expected return and minimize risk, subject to various linear constraints. The underlying optimization issues in both cases are those illustrated in Exhibits 1.1 and 2.2. There are, however, some noteworthy differences between asset allocation and equity portfolio optimizations.

In an asset allocation study, the number of risky assets rarely exceeds 50 and is typically in the range of 3–20. The number of optimization constraints is often relatively minimal. The assets generally include broad asset categories, such as U.S. equities and corporate and government bonds, international equities and bonds, real estate, and venture capital. Sample means, variances, and correlations, based on monthly, quarterly, or annual historic data, may serve as starting points for optimization input estimates.[11] In a benchmark-relative framework such as that shown in Exhibit 2.2, the residual return basis for optimization inputs often equals the difference between historic asset and index returns.

For equity portfolio management, benchmark optimization (see Exhibit 2.2) is generally the framework of choice. This is true because the measure of investment performance for institutional equity management is almost always benchmark-relative. The benchmark return is usually related to the return of a representative market index.

An equity portfolio optimization generally includes many securities. Domestic equity optimizations typically include 100–500 stocks. International equity optimizations may include as many as 4,000–5,000 stocks. Equity portfolio optimizations usually include many constraints on portfolio characteristics, industry or sector membership, and trading cost restrictions.

The source of equity optimization inputs is normally very different from those in an asset allocation. Sample means and covariances of historic returns are typically not the starting points for inputs in an equity portfolio optimization. Modern financial theory provides a rich framework for defining expected and residual return for equities.[12] In equilibrium, the expected return of a security is a function of its systematic risk. High expected return may indicate high systematic risk and not mispricing. The estimate of expected return associated with systematic risk generally derives from some version of the Capital Asset Pricing Model or Arbitrage Pricing Theory.[13]

---

[11] See chapters 8–11 for further discussion of input estimation.

[12] The two most influential modern financial theories of stock pricing are the Sharpe (1964)-Lintner (1965) capital asset pricing model (CAPM) and the Ross (1975, 1976) arbitrage pricing theory (APT).

[13] Commercial services may use a compromise version of an "expanded" or multi-beta CAPM that is similar to an APT framework to define systematic risk.

Equity risk models provide useful estimates of the components of stock and portfolio residual risk shown in Exhibit 2.2. In practice, institutional asset managers often use commercial risk measurement services to estimate security and portfolio residual risk. Over- and underpricing are associated with α, or expected return net of systematic risk expected return. The process of defining α for equity portfolio optimization is often a major undertaking and may be the primary investment focus of an equity management firm. Many institutional asset managers employ stock valuation procedures based on sophisticated econometric analysis and techniques.[14]

Another common application of MV optimizers for equity portfolio management is to define a tracking or index fund.[15] In this case, α is zero, and the optimizer finds the minimum risk-tracking portfolio given the constraints. Without constraints or trading costs, the minimum tracking fund is the index. For tracking funds, the efficient frontier shown in Exhibit 2.2 reduces to a point on the x-axis near or at the origin.

For equity portfolios, estimation of α and security and portfolio residual risk, portfolio constraints, trading costs, the number of assets, and other issues of practical importance substantially increase the complexity of the optimization process. In contrast, asset allocation typically reflects a much simpler and more convenient framework for the study of MV optimization.

## A Global Asset Allocation Example

Consider a global asset manager allocating capital to the following eight major asset classes: U.S. stocks and government/corporate bonds, Euros, and the Canadian, French, German, Japanese, and U.K. equity markets. The historic data consists of 216 months of index total returns in U.S. dollars for all eight asset classes and for U.S. 30-day T-

---

[14] For a recent example see Michaud 1998.

[15] An index fund is a portfolio designed to track an index. One simple method for defining an index fund is to include all the stocks in the index with index weights as portfolio weights. In this case, optimization is not required. Optimizers may be useful when constraints are required or liquidity issues are important.

[16] The data for five equity markets—Canada, France, Germany, Japan, and United Kingdom—are Morgan Stanley Capital International U.S. dollar total return indices net of withholding taxes. The U.S. equity data is S&P 500 Index total returns. The 30-day T-bill returns are from Salomon Brothers. The two bond data indices are the Lehman Brothers government/corporate U.S. bond index and U.S. dollar Eurobond global index. The Lehman Brothers Eurobond Global Index was available from January 1978 to November 1994. The Eurobond returns for the remaining months were from Lehman Brothers Eurobond Global Issues Index. The limited availability of long-term Eurobond returns governed the choice of time period used in this example.

**Table 2.1:** Monthly Dollars (Net) Returns (Percentages),
January 1978–December 1995

|  | Mean | Standard Deviation |
|---|---|---|
| Canada | 0.97 | 5.47 |
| France | 1.46 | 7.00 |
| Germany | 1.11 | 6.19 |
| Japan | 1.46 | 7.01 |
| U.K. | 1.37 | 5.99 |
| U.S. | 1.29 | 4.28 |
| U.S. Bonds | 0.83 | 1.99 |
| Euros | 0.85 | 1.52 |

*Note:* U.S. 30-day T-bill return mean = 0.58%; standard deviation = 0.24%.

bills, from January 1978 through December 1995.[16] Table 2.1 provides the averages and standard deviations of the monthly data for the assets in this period.

Quadratic programming finds the optimal MV efficient frontier asset allocations under the assumptions. Exhibit 2.3 displays the efficient frontier for the usual constraints.[17] The graph displays annualized data.[18] The exhibit includes plots and labels of the means and standard deviations of the eight assets.

---

[17] Computing and displaying the efficient frontier in Exhibit 2.3, and in subsequent examples of efficient frontiers, means computing and displaying a set of points representing the mean and standard deviation of a representative set of efficient portfolios. The procedure used computes 51 efficient portfolios, ranging from minimum variance to maximum expected return portfolios. In general, the points chosen are equally spaced along the return axis of the efficient frontier. The exception to this rule is for the last five efficient portfolios at the high-return end of the efficient frontier, where the standard deviation changes rapidly relative to changes in expected return. In this case, very small changes in return map out the upper range of the efficient frontier.

[18] Twelve multiplies the average monthly returns, and the square root of 12 multiplies the monthly return standard deviations.

**Exhibit 2.3:** Classic Mean-Variance Efficient Frontier

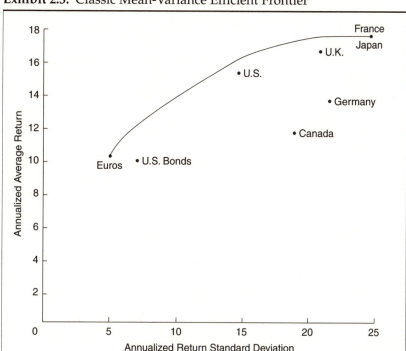

Because the French stock market index had the highest average monthly return, it is on the efficient frontier at the most northeast point of the curve. The Japanese market had nearly the same return and risk, and its plot in Exhibit 2.3 is virtually indistinguishable from that of France. The minimum risk portfolio is more than 98% Euros, with 0.86% average monthly return and 1.52% monthly standard deviation. Other points on the efficient frontier lie between these two extremes. For example, the efficient frontier asset allocation with average monthly return 1.24% and standard deviation 3.33% (roughly halfway between the largest and smallest return efficient portfolios) is composed of approximately 10% French, 20% Japanese, 5% U.K., and 45% U.S. equities and 20% Euros. U.S. bonds significantly underperformed all other assets and an efficient portfolio for its level of risk. In Exhibit 2.3, it is clear that the French, Japanese, U.K., and U.S. equity markets as well as Euros are near or on the efficient frontier and performed well relative to their level of risk in this time period. For many levels of risk, however, diversification was useful.

## Reference Portfolios and Portfolio Analysis

Reference portfolios are often helpful in understanding the investment meaning of efficient frontiers. They serve as useful guideposts for comparing the implications of alternative portfolios. Table 2.2 defines three reference portfolios used in subsequent analyses of MV portfolio efficiency: index, current, and equal-weighted. The index portfolio is roughly consistent with a capitalization-weighted portfolio relative to a world equity benchmark for the six equity markets. The current portfolio represents a typical U.S.–based investor's global portfolio asset allocation. The most significant differences between the index and current portfolios are the allocations to fixed income assets. An equal-weighted portfolio is useful as a reference point.

Exhibit 2.4 provides the results of including the reference portfolios in the efficient frontier analysis. All the reference portfolios plot close to the efficient frontier and appear reasonably well diversified.

## Return Premium Efficient Frontiers

The return premium is the return minus the risk-free rate. It is often convenient to use total return premiums, instead of total returns, as the basis of MV analysis in practice. Return premiums are similar to real rates of return. By removing the impact of varying risk-free rates, return premiums may be relatively more stable than total returns and more useful in a forecasting context.

The total return premium is the U.S. dollar total return minus the U.S. dollar short-term interest rate in each period. The monthly short-term interest rate for a U.S. dollar–based investor is usually defined as the U.S. T-bill 30-day return. Table 2.3 displays the mean and standard deviation of the total monthly return premiums over the January 1978–December 1995 period for the eight assets in Table 2.1. Table 2.4 provides the correlations. The data in Tables 2.3 and 2.4 give a complete description of the input parameters required for MV optimization.

Exhibit 2.5 displays the MV efficient frontier associated with the historic return premium data. Exhibit 2.5 and Tables 2.3 and 2.4 are the basis of most of the examples illustrated in the text.

**Table 2.2:** Reference Portfolios (Percentages)

|  | Index | Current | Equal |
|---|---|---|---|
| Canada | 5 | 5 | 12.5 |
| France | 10 | 10 | 12.5 |
| Germany | 10 | 0 | 12.5 |
| Japan | 30 | 20 | 12.5 |
| U.K. | 10 | 15 | 12.5 |
| U.S. | 35 | 20 | 12.5 |
| U.S. Bonds | 0 | 20 | 12.5 |
| Euros | 0 | 5 | 12.5 |

**Table 2.3:** Monthly Dollar (Net) Return Premium (Percentages), January 1978–December 1995

|  | Mean | Standard Deviation |
|---|---|---|
| Canada | 0.39 | 5.50 |
| France | 0.88 | 7.03 |
| Germany | 0.53 | 6.22 |
| Japan | 0.88 | 7.04 |
| U.K. | 0.79 | 6.01 |
| U.S. | 0.71 | 4.30 |
| U.S. Bonds | 0.25 | 2.01 |
| Euros | 0.27 | 1.56 |

**Exhibit 2.4:** Classic Efficient Frontier with Reference Portfolios

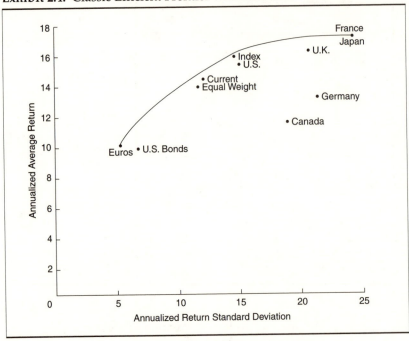

**Exhibit 2.5:** Mean-Variance Return Premium Efficient
Frontier

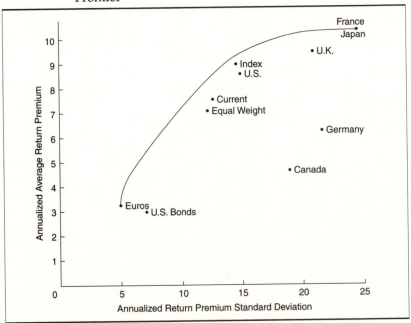

**Table 2.4:** Asset Correlations: Monthly Dollars (Net) Return Premium, January 1978–December 1995

|  | Canada | France | Germany | Japan | U.K. | U.S. | U.S. Bonds | Euros |
|---|---|---|---|---|---|---|---|---|
| Canada | 1.00 | 0.41 | 0.30 | 0.25 | 0.58 | 0.71 | 0.26 | 0.33 |
| France | 0.41 | 1.00 | 0.62 | 0.42 | 0.54 | 0.44 | 0.22 | 0.26 |
| Germany | 0.30 | 0.62 | 1.00 | 0.35 | 0.48 | 0.34 | 0.27 | 0.28 |
| Japan | 0.25 | 0.42 | 0.35 | 1.00 | 0.40 | 0.22 | 0.14 | 0.16 |
| U.K. | 0.58 | 0.54 | 0.48 | 0.40 | 1.00 | 0.56 | 0.25 | 0.29 |
| U.S. | 0.71 | 0.44 | 0.34 | 0.22 | 0.56 | 1.00 | 0.36 | 0.42 |
| U.S. Bonds | 0.26 | 0.22 | 0.27 | 0.14 | 0.25 | 0.36 | 1.00 | 0.92 |
| Euros | 0.33 | 0.26 | 0.28 | 0.16 | 0.29 | 0.42 | 0.92 | 1.00 |

*Appendix*

# Mathematical Formulation of Mean-Variance Efficiency

## Mean-Variance Efficiency

Let

$N$ = number of assets or securities in the universe

$w$ = vector of portfolio weights of the $N$ assets

$\mu$ = vector of expected returns of the $N$ assets

$\Sigma$ = covariance matrix of the $N$ assets

$\mathbf{1}$ = vector of ones of length $N$.

By definition, the mean and variance of a portfolio $P$ with weights $w_p$ is:

$$\mu_p = w_p{'} * \mu$$

$$\sigma_p^2 = w_p{'} * \Sigma * w_p$$

where $w'$ denotes the transpose of the vector $w$.

Portfolio $P$ is MV efficient for a given level of portfolio expected return $\mu^*$ if it satisfies the following conditions:

minimize $w_p{'} * \Sigma * w_p$

subject to the constraint $w_p{'} * \mu = \mu^*$.

In many cases of practical interest, MV efficient portfolio weights are further constrained to sum to 1,

$$w_p{'} * \mathbf{1} = 1$$

and to have nonnegative values

$$w \geq 0.$$

## Parametric Quadratic Programming and Mean-Variance Efficiency

"Parametric" quadratic programming is a useful alternative formulation of MV efficiency. In this case, a parameter $\lambda$ (lambda) is introduced into the description of the optimization. The condition that identifies the efficient portfolios is to minimize $\phi$ (phi):

$$\phi = \sigma_p^2 - \lambda\mu_p$$

for a given value of $\lambda$ subject to the associated linear equality and inequality constraints. This formulation of MV optimization leads to efficient computation of the entire MV efficient frontier.[19]

To show how this works, it is convenient to introduce the concept of a "pivot point" or "corner portfolio" on the efficient frontier. Technically, corner portfolios are efficient frontier portfolios that represent transition points, where at least one of the inequalities in the optimization either becomes binding or is no longer binding on the solution. Less technically, a corner portfolio is an efficient portfolio in which an asset either enters or leaves the set of efficient portfolios in a neighborhood of the corner portfolio.[20]

Corner portfolios are important for computing the efficient frontier due to the following technical property: If $w^*$ and $w^{**}$ are vectors representing weights of portfolios on the efficient frontier, then a portfolio formed from the convex sum of the two portfolios—$c^*w^* + (1 - c)^*w^{**}$, $0 \leq c \leq 1$—is also an MV efficient portfolio if no corner portfolio exists between $w^*$ and $w^{**}$. Consequently, the efficient frontier between $w^*$ and $w^{**}$ is computable simply from knowing the composition of two distinct efficient portfolios, when corner portfolios do not exist between them. Parametric quadratic procedures find the values of $\lambda$ associated with the corner portfolios. It is therefore possible to compute all corner portfolios and thereby the entire efficient frontier exactly and efficiently using parametric quadratic programming methods. This approach is often more efficient than simply computing a large number of portfolios across the length of the efficient frontier.

Parametric quadratic programming is conceptually interesting because it provides a deeper understanding of the nature of the efficient

---

[19] Early successful parametric quadratic programming methods include the critical-line algorithm of Markowitz (1956) and Beale (1955). For an extensive up-to-date discussion of the critical line algorithm, see Markowitz (1987). Computational methods based on the simplex algorithm include Beale (1959), Frank and Wolfe (1956), and Wolfe (1959).

[20] See Sharpe (1970) for a leisurely exposition.

frontier. In many practical applications, however, computing efficient portfolios at specific values of portfolio expected return or risk is often of primary interest, and parametric quadratic programming of the efficient frontier is a luxury.

## Exact versus Approximate Mean-Variance Optimizers

The choice of an MV optimization algorithm may often depend on the computational speed and accuracy required. In cases such as equity portfolio optimization, only a single point on the efficient frontier may be of interest and an approximate optimal solution may be sufficient. In many cases, commercial equity portfolio optimizers optimize computational speed using algorithms that are single-point approximations to efficient frontier portfolios. However, when practical, quadratic programming algorithms that compute exact solutions remain the algorithms of choice. Useful enhancements are available for the exact quadratic programming solution of relatively large-scale optimization problems in the presence of factor models (Perold 1984). In addition, recent developments in computational power and algorithmic sophistication may soon eliminate many of the practical benefits of approximate optimization algorithms, even for large international equity portfolios.

# Chapter 3

# Traditional Criticisms
# and Alternatives

*M*any authors have raised serious objections to mean-variance (MV) efficiency as a framework for defining portfolio optimality and have proposed a number of alternatives. Most of the alternatives can be classified in one of five categories: (1) nonvariance risk measures, (2) utility function optimization, (3) multiperiod objectives, (4) Monte Carlo financial planning, or (5) linear programming. Analysis shows that the alternatives often have their own serious limitations and that MV efficiency is far more robust than is appreciated. Although they are symptomatic of an underlying unease with MV efficiency, none of the proposals address the basic limitations of MV optimization.

## Alternative Measures of Risk

In MV efficiency, the variance, or standard deviation, of return is the measure of security and portfolio risk. The variance measures variability above and below the mean. From an investor's point of view, the variance of returns above the mean is often not "risk." One obvious and intuitively appealing nonvariance measure of risk, discussed as early as Markowitz (1959), is the semivariance or semistandard deviation of return. In this risk measure, only returns below the mean are included in the estimate of variability.

The semivariance is an example of a "downside" risk measure. In this case, "downside" risk is relative to the average or mean of return. There are many other ways to measure "downside" risk. A simple example is replacing average return with a specified level of return, such as zero or the risk-free rate.

Many other nonvariance measures of variability are also available. Some of the more important include the mean absolute deviation and range measures. The pros and cons of various risk measures depend on the nature of the return distribution.

The return distribution of an asset or portfolio depends on several factors. Because the returns of diversified equity portfolios, equity indexes, and other assets are often approximately symmetric over periods of institutional interest, efficiency based on nonvariance risk measures may be nearly equivalent to MV efficiency.

An important issue is whether, in practice, nonvariance risk measures lead to significantly different efficient portfolios. Exhibit 3.1 provides an illustration, comparing the MV efficient frontier in Exhibit 2.5 with a mean-semivariance efficient frontier based on the same historic data. As Exhibit 3.1 shows, the two efficient frontiers are virtually identical, except at the low-risk end. The differences at low risk reflect the fact that bond returns are less symmetric than equities. Many currently fashionable risk alternatives have similar efficient frontier characteristics.

Some asset classes, such as options, do not have return distributions that are approximately symmetric. The return distributions of

**Exhibit 3.1:** Mean-Variance and Semi-Variance Efficient Frontiers

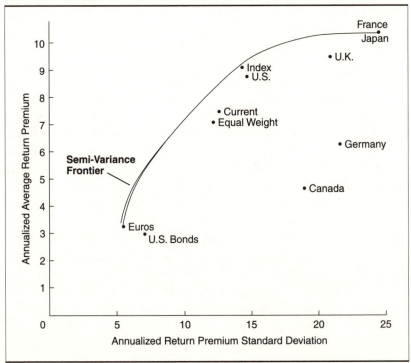

fixed-income indexes are not as symmetric as many equity asset classes. In addition, the return distribution of diversified equity portfolios becomes increasingly asymmetric over a long-enough period. Consequently, the variance measure for defining portfolio efficiency is not always useful or appropriate. For many applications of institutional interest, however, a variance-based efficient frontier is often little different (and even less often statistically significantly different) from frontiers that use other measures of risk. It is also generally a lot more convenient, especially when deriving statistical properties of efficient frontiers, as is done later in the book.

## Utility Function Optimization

For many financial economists, maximizing expected utility of terminal wealth is the basis for all rational decision making under uncertainty. The issue of interest is whether Markowitz MV efficiency is consistent with expected utility maximization. If it is not, perhaps optimization based on specific utility functions should replace MV efficiency.

Markowitz MV efficiency is strictly consistent with expected utility maximization only under either of two conditions: normally distributed asset returns or quadratic utility functions. The normal distribution assumption is unacceptable to most analysts and investors. Although diversified equity portfolio and index returns are often reasonably symmetric, their distribution is not precisely normal. In addition, the limitations of quadratic utility as a representation of investor behavior are well known.[1] Consequently, MV efficiency is not strictly consistent with expected utility maximization.

One alternative is to define portfolio optimality in terms of optimizing specific utility functions. Many analysts have suggested that utility functions are a more rational basis for investor decision making and portfolio structuring. Utility function optimizations need not resemble MV efficient portfolios.

There are, however, significant practical limitations to using utility functions as the basis of defining an optimization. One obvious limitation is the feasibility and viability of practical algorithms for computing optimal portfolios. Depending on functional form, nonlinear

---

[1] Because a quadratic function is not monotone increasing as a function of wealth, from some point on, expected quadratic utility declines as a function of increasing wealth. Quadratic utility functions are primarily useful as approximations of expected utility maximization, usually in some particular region of the wealth spectrum.

optimization methods may be required that may have significant limitations in many applications.

An equally important limitation of the utility function approach to portfolio optimization is utility function specificity. In practice, investor utility is unknown. The lack of specificity of the investor's utility function is a far more daunting practical problem than it may appear. This is because a class of utility functions can have similar functional forms, perhaps differing in the value of only one or two parameters, yet represent a very wide, even contradictory, spectrum of risk bearing and investment behavior (Rubinstein 1973). In these cases, even small errors in the estimation of utility function parameters can lead to very large changes in the investment characteristics of an optimal portfolio. As a practical matter, the problem of specifying with sufficient accuracy the appropriate utility function for a given investor appears to be a severe practical limitation of utility function–based portfolio optimization.

On the other hand, MV efficiency is rationalizable as a convenient approximation of expected utility maximization. For nonpathologic utility functions, quadratic utility functions are often useful approximations of maximum expected utility at a point.[2] Note that the best-approximating quadratic function may not be the same at different points of the expected utility function. Consequently, MV efficient portfolios are often good approximations of maximum expected utility and a practical framework for portfolio optimization (Levy and Markowitz 1979; Kroll, Levy, and Markowitz 1984; Markowitz 1987, ch. 3).

The use of utility functions in defining portfolio optimality often divides practitioners from academics. From a rigorous point of view, only the specification of an appropriate utility function will do for defining portfolio optimality. However, few practitioners use nonquadratic utility functions to find optimal portfolios. Given the difficulty of estimating utility functions with sufficient precision, the convenience of quadratic programming algorithms, and the robustness of the approximating power of quadratic utility at a point, MV efficiency is often the practical tool of choice.

## Multiperiod Investment Horizons

Markowitz MV efficiency is formally a single-period model for investment behavior. Many institutional investors, however, such as endowment and pension funds, have long-term investment horizons on

---

[2] The result is Taylor's theorem for a continuous and sufficiently smooth utility function.

the order of 5, 10, or 20 years. How useful is MV efficiency for investors with long-term investment objectives?

One way to address long-term objectives is to base MV efficiency analysis on long-term units of time. MV efficiency, however, is probably most appropriate for relatively short-term periods. This is true because a quadratic approximation of maximum expected utility is most likely to be valid for monthly, quarterly, or yearly periods. In addition, lengthening the unit of time reduces the number of independent periods in a historic data set and the statistical significance of optimization parameter estimates. On the other hand, increasing the historic data period may diminish the relevance of the estimates for the forecast period.

An alternative approach is to consider the multiperiod distribution of the geometric mean of return. The geometric mean, or compound, return is the statistic of choice for summarizing portfolio return over multiple periods.[3]

Assume that, in each period, MV efficiency defines optimal portfolio choice. Also assume that the distribution of single-period return does not vary (appreciably) over the multiperiod investment horizon. What are the long-term consequences of repeatedly investing in MV efficient portfolios?

Some essential results are due to Markowitz (1959, ch. 6). He shows that (1) MV efficient portfolios need not be efficient in the long run, and (2) long-term efficiency is not necessarily monotonic in portfolio risk. In particular, MV efficient portfolios on the upper segment of the efficient frontier may be less long-term efficient than portfolios with less risk.[4]

Hakansson (1971a) gives an example of an MV efficient frontier in which repeated investing produces a negative long-term geometric mean at all points. This example shows that all MV efficient frontier portfolios may lead to ruin with probability equal to 1 over long-enough investment horizons. However, the Hakansson example is neither typical nor likely.

Further analysis of the geometric mean criterion is useful.[5] The mean and variance of $N$-period geometric mean return is a natural

---

[3] Suppose an investor experiences a 100% return in one period and a –50% return in the next period. The two-period average return is 25%, but the two-period wealth is the same as at the beginning. Therefore, the true multiperiod return is 0%. The geometric mean provides the correct answer, whereas the average does not.

[4] Markowitz' use of the phrases "return in the long run" and "long-term return" refer to the almost sure limit of geometric mean return as the number of periods becomes large.

[5] Much of the following discussion follows Michaud 1981.

*N*-period generalization of Markowitz efficiency.[6] Various approximations show that portfolios on the (single-period) MV efficient frontier are often good approximations of *N*-period geometric mean efficient portfolios.[7] Consequently, *N*-period geometric mean MV efficiency is roughly a special case of MV efficiency in many cases of practical interest.

Define the critical point as the MV efficient portfolio with the maximum *N*-period expected geometric mean return. The critical point is a useful construct for understanding and using *N*-period geometric mean efficiency. The *N*-period expected geometric mean is a positive function of the mean of (single-period) expected return and a negative function of the variance. Consequently, the critical point defines the boundary of portfolios on the lower segment of the MV efficient frontier that are *N*-period geometric mean MV efficient and those on the upper segment that are not. *N*-period horizon MV efficiency leads to the simple decision rule of considering only MV efficient portfolios on the lower segment of the efficient frontier up to the critical point efficient portfolio.[8] Note that critical points that are not end points of the MV efficient frontier do not always exist.

A number of analysts have raised objections to the geometric mean as an investment criterion. In particular, a significant controversy emerged from the proposal of using the (long-term) expected geometric mean as a surrogate for expected utility (Hakansson 1971b). This controversy, although it is beyond the scope of this discussion, is essentially concerned with the limitations of using any investment rule, however attractive, as an alternative to expected utility maximization. The opposing view concerns the limitations of using utility functions in practice and the value of the MV geometric mean criterion as a convenient source of useful investment information.[9] MV geometric mean investment objectives are often consistent with many institutional investment mandates.

---

[6] It may be fitting to call the objective Hakansson efficiency, after the researcher who has done much of the pioneering work in this area.

[7] For example, Young and Trent (1969) and Michaud (1981, appendix). Approximation accuracy depends on assumptions that are often satisfied in practical applications.

[8] One simple procedure is to find the MV efficient portfolio with the maximum value of an MV approximation to the *N*-period geometric mean using a search algorithm of all portfolios on the efficient frontier. Michaud (1981) provides three analytic formulas for estimating the efficient frontier critical point for the special case of portfolios on the Capital Asset Pricing Model (CAPM) market line.

[9] See Markowitz (1976) and Michaud (1981) for further discussion and many additional references.

One more issue may be of interest. The assumption has been that the investor repeatedly invests in the same efficient frontier portfolio over some investment horizon. However, optimal multiperiod investment with an MV geometric mean objective is a dynamic programming strategy that implies varying the choices of MV efficient portfolios in each period (Michaud and Monahan 1981).

Multiperiod considerations are important issues for investors with long-term investment objectives. To avoid possible negative long-term consequences of MV efficiency, a simple solution is to limit consideration to efficient frontier portfolios at or below the critical point. As a useful approximation, it is convenient to consider long-term efficient portfolios as a subset and a special case of MV efficiency.

## Asset-Liability Financial Planning Studies

Many financial institutions invest substantial resources in defining an appropriate long-term average asset allocation or investment policy.[10] They do this because the long-term average asset allocation is one of the most important investment decisions an institution or investor can make.[11] The importance of defining an optimal investment policy has spurred alternative approaches to MV efficiency analysis. Probably the most important of these is an asset-liability financial planning study based on Monte Carlo simulation.

In a Monte Carlo financial planning study, a computer model simulates the random functioning of a fund and changes in its liabilities over time.[12] Estimates of likely cash flows and funding status result from performing many simulations. By varying asset return and allocation assumptions, the simulation can evaluate the implications of various asset allocation decisions on the evolution of funding status

---

[10] Such projects can involve a number of consultants and substantial expenditures.

[11] There is a significant controversy on the degree of importance of the long-term asset allocation decision. Some authors (e.g., Brinson, Hood, and Beebower 1986) argue that the long-term asset allocation may account for more than 90% of investment results. More recent studies (e.g., Hensel, Ezra, and Ilkiw 1991) find that investment policy, active asset allocation, and active stock selection are roughly equally comparable in importance. At a minimum, most analysts agree that investment policy is at least as important as any other class of investment decisions.

[12] Depending on the study and application, the liability model may be very detailed. For a defined benefit pension plan, it can include a comprehensive examination of corporate objectives, economic projections, and future hiring policy as well as current workforce census. In some cases, liability modeling may affect asset allocation decisions in terms of feasibility, particularly for regulated firms, such as insurance companies.

and cash flows. Endowment fund simulations can provide useful information on likely levels of endowment spending and fund value over time. Similarly, defined benefit pension plan simulations can be useful for anticipating required contributions and plan funding status for various assumptions and investment periods.[13]

The important issue is whether Monte Carlo asset-liability financial planning is a superior alternative to MV efficiency for defining an optimal asset allocation. Proponents argue that plan funding status and cash flow objectives are more meaningful than the MV efficiency of a feasible portfolio. The anticipation of likely cash flows and required contributions can provide valuable fund planning information. The problem is that such information may have relatively limited usefulness for defining an optimal long-term asset allocation.

Generally, only feasible MV efficient frontier asset allocations relative to fund liability are of interest.[14] This is because feasible liability-relative allocations with more expected return for a given risk level are almost always preferable. Consequently, a valid Monte Carlo asset-liability simulation study still requires liability-relative MV efficiency analysis to determine candidate efficient allocations. Within the context of feasible liability-relative efficient allocations, consider the consequences of varying asset mixes. In general, the Monte Carlo results show that riskier efficient asset mixes lead to a greater likelihood of meeting or exceeding funding objectives and of increasing volatility. Evaluating the tradeoffs associated with funding status and cash flow volatility in various time periods is often of no less difficulty than evaluating the risk-return tradeoffs in an efficient frontier context. Monte Carlo simulation studies do little more than illustrate the simple principle that, for feasible efficient portfolios, more risk leads to more return on average, and more volatility.

There is an exception to these basic principles governing Monte Carlo asset-liability financial planning simulation. Analysts have seen that increasing efficient portfolio risk does not always lead to an increased likelihood of meeting fund objectives. Such results appear to rationalize the importance of the Monte Carlo procedure relative to efficiency analysis. However, the discussion in the previous section of this chapter can help to explain this result.

---

[13] Michaud (1976) provides a detailed example of the Monte Carlo financial planning process for defined benefit pension plans.

[14] See chapter 10 for further discussion of benchmark liability-relative MV efficiency.

Monte Carlo simulation studies generally assume repeated investment in candidate portfolios. If the liability-relative efficient frontier has an internal critical point, asset allocations on the long-term inefficient segment will exhibit the behavior that increasing risk leads to decreases in the ability of the fund to meet objectives. In many cases, such results are analytically anticipatable by computing the critical point of the efficient frontier (or of the candidate portfolios) and analyzing $N$-period geometric mean efficiency. However, the issue is more than simply a tool for rationalizing the results of a simulation study. The $N$-period geometric mean implications of input assumptions are the engine that drives the simulations and can lead to predefined conclusions.

Monte Carlo asset-liability simulation has many uses as a tool for financial planning. It is useful for understanding the likelihood of meeting funding objectives and likely cash flows associated with various fund investments and allocations. The procedure has limited value, however, as an alternative to MV efficiency for defining an optimal asset allocation. Many of its asset allocation benefits are analytically anticipatable in terms of the mean and variance of the multiperiod geometric mean distribution. On the other hand, the analytic tools for understanding the geometric mean distribution as a function of the MV efficient frontier portfolios over an $N$-period investment horizon can be useful for designing effective Monte Carlo simulation financial planning studies (Michaud 1981).

## Linear Programming Optimization

The practical limitations of MV optimization as a tool of equity portfolio management have been familiar to many astute asset managers for many years. One common alternative is to optimize portfolios with linear programming.[15]

Linear programming portfolio optimization is a special case of quadratic programming. The most significant difference is that linear programming does not include portfolio variance. In this procedure, the objective is to maximize expected equity portfolio return subject to a variety of linear equality and inequality constraints on portfolio structure. The procedure relies heavily on clever use of constraints on industries, sectors, and stock weights to control portfolio risk and

---

[15] See, for example, Farrell (1983) 168–74.

maximize expected return. The constraints also serve to design portfolios with various specific characteristics and objectives.

In the hands of a sophisticated analyst, linear programming is an optimization technique that may avoid many of the fundamental limitations of equity portfolio MV optimization. It has its own limitations, however. In practice, it is difficult to control the structure of a portfolio precisely. From a theoretical point of view, only an MV optimization framework can optimally use active forecast information (Sharpe 1985, 666–70). The issue remains whether any linear programming approach is to be preferred to a carefully defined, input-adjusted, MV optimization. The problems that most limit the practical value of MV optimization may be more attributable to the return than to risk dimension, which suggests that the linear programming alternative may ultimately be of limited value.

A somewhat obvious final issue may be worthy of note. Several investment institutions use far less sophisticated optimization procedures than linear or quadratic programming.[16] These "homemade" optimization alternatives are often not the product of a conscious effort to avoid MV optimizer limitations but reflect a lack of analytic sophistication in the organization. Technical limitations in an optimization algorithm are unlikely to enhance the investment value of a portfolio over standard procedures.

---

[16] Linear programming generally finds exact solutions under the assumptions. However, some institutions use optimization approximations that may have additional limitations.

# Chapter 4

# Understanding Mean-Variance Efficiency

*M*ean-variance (MV) optimization has severe limitations as a tool of investment management. Some limitations can be explained by various institutional practices, including suboptimal input estimation, incomplete or inappropriate optimization frameworks, poorly constructed forecasts, and errors caused by misunderstanding how optimization algorithms work. These and related subjects are addressed in subsequent chapters. This chapter describes and addresses the implications of the fundamental limitations of MV efficiency for practical investment management and provides a context for many of the tools that follow.

## The Fundamental Limitations of Mean-Variance Efficiency

The most serious practical limitations of MV efficiency are instability and ambiguity. Small changes in input assumptions often lead to large changes in the optimized portfolio. Anecdotally, many investment practitioners have known of the instability and ambiguity of MV optimization and the unintuitive investment character of optimized portfolios since quadratic programming procedures became available.[1] The operative question is not whether MV optimizations are unstable or unintuitive, but rather, how serious is the problem? Unfortunately, for many investment applications, it is very serious indeed.

J.D. Jobson and Bob Korkie wrote the classic pioneering studies on the instability and ambiguity of MV optimization and its invest-

---

[1] The author began using the MIT-Rand QP (parametric quadratic programming) Fortran subroutine in investment research in 1973.

ment implications. In 1980, they made asymptotic analytic estimates of the biases produced by MV optimizers and showed that the biases can be very large. In 1981, they used Monte Carlo techniques to simulate the behavior of an MV optimizer.[2] For a given set of historic data for 20 stocks and 60-month estimation periods, they found that the simulated MV efficient frontiers had an average maximum Sharpe ratio of 0.08.[3] This result contrasts with the true Sharpe ratio for the data (0.32) and the Sharpe ratio of an equal-weighted portfolio (0.27). The Jobson and Korkie results put to rest the fallacy that MV optimized portfolios are somehow better than others even though they are difficult to understand. MV optimized portfolios are hard to understand because they often do not make investment sense and do not have investment value.

Proper interpretation of the implications of Jobson and Korkie's results for institutional asset management requires an important qualification. Their optimized portfolios are not sign-constrained. Most institutional equity portfolios are short-selling–constrained. As demonstrated in the next section, a short-selling constraint significantly reduces the magnitude of the poor performance of optimized portfolios. Consequently, typical institutional portfolios moderate, but do not invalidate, the Jobson and Korkie results. Their results also show the importance of imposing financially meaningful constraints on the optimization process when available.[4]

---

[2] The Jobson and Korkie Monte Carlo simulation experiment is an example of data resampling, or bootstrapping. Data resampling methods have become increasingly important in modern statistics. See Judge et al. (1988, 416–19), for a brief overview and Efron and Tibshirani (1993) for a comprehensive authoritative description. One important reason that simulation is so useful is that it can represent an out-of-sample test of the investment performance of MV optimized portfolios assuming that the inputs are relevant for the investment horizon of interest. Alternative methods generally have to deal with the additional issue of changes in the underlying return distribution.

[3] Jobson and Korkie's (1981) Monte Carlo simulation procedure is as follows: A set of means, standard deviations, and correlations of monthly returns for 20 stocks, estimated over some historic period, is assumed to be the true state of nature. Monte Carlo simulations of the historic data simulate 60- or 100-month returns for each asset. From the simulated returns, compute the simulated optimization inputs—means, standard deviations and correlations of the 20 stocks—and associated efficient frontier maximum Sharpe ratio portfolios. Repeat this procedure many times. Because the simulated data has statistical error, each simulated efficient frontier is unlikely to be the true efficient frontier, and the estimated maximum Sharpe ratio portfolio varies with each simulation. Now compare the average Sharpe ratio for the simulated maximum Sharpe ratio portfolio to the actual maximum Sharpe ratio and the Sharpe ratio of an equal-weighted portfolio for the historic data.

[4] This is the recommendation in Frost and Savarino (1988).

## Repeating Jobson and Korkie

To provide a baseline for the results that follow, it is useful to repeat the Jobson and Korkie experiment for the data in Tables 2.3 and 2.4.[5,6] For sign unconstrained portfolios, the true maximum Sharpe ratio for the data is 0.253.[7] Replicating the 216-month historic return estimation period, the average of the Sharpe ratios for 500 simulations of the eight-asset data is 0.200.[8] This value is 20% less than the true value.

Jobson and Korkie use 100-month and 60-month estimation periods. Replicating Jobson and Korkie with 500 simulations and the eight-asset data, the average Sharpe ratios for 100 estimation periods is 0.157 and for 60 periods is 0.128.[9] The results show that shorter estimation periods have a significant impact on increasing estimation error and reducing the average performance of optimized portfolios, all other things being the same.

Although the simulations find serious degradation in average investment performance for sign unconstrained optimized portfolios with the eight-asset data, the results are not as negative as those found by Jobson and Korkie. Apart from the data itself, the smaller number

---

[5] Jobson and Korkie (1981) use the following formula for computing the simulated maximum Sharpe ratio portfolios: *smean*\**inv*(*scov*), where *smean* is the row vector for the Monte Carlo simulated means and *inv*(*scov*) is the inverse of the simulated covariance matrix. The reward-to-risk ratio using the means and covariances of Tables 2.3 and 2.4 is the measure of the performance of the simulated Sharpe ratio optimal portfolios. The simulated portfolios in this case are not short-selling–constrained. The simulated portfolios produced by the formula are unlikely to satisfy the budget constraint. Dividing the portfolio weights by the portfolio sum normalizes the portfolio so that it satisfies the budget constraint. However, the reward-to-risk ratio before and after normalization may be different if the sum of the weights is negative. The alternative used here is to ignore simulated portfolios when the sum of the weights is negative.

[6] The simulated returns are multivariate normally distributed. The algorithm used in the results reported is mvnrnd.m, from MathWorks. Tests using nonparametric (bootstrapping) and parametric (multivariate normal) resampling found results that were essentially the same.

[7] Note that for return premium data, the portfolio Sharpe ratio is the same as the reward-to-risk ratio and is equal to the portfolio mean divided by the standard deviation.

[8] The distribution of the reward-to-risk ratios of the simulated portfolios is of investment interest. The fifth-percentile maximum Sharpe ratio is 0.138, the ninety-fifth percentile is 0.238, the minimum value is 0.088, and the maximum value is 0.248. The Sharpe ratios have a skew value of –1.08, indicating that, when error maximization negatively affects the optimized portfolio, the effect may be very serious. The relatively large skew value is a function of the small number of assets in the example. Larger numbers of assets lead to less skew in the distribution of the maximum Sharpe ratios, all other things being equal.

[9] The reported numbers are an average of the results of four 500 resampling simulations. There was negligible variance in the estimates.

of assets also helps to reduce the amount of error maximization observed relative to Jobson and Korkie's study.

## Implications of Jobson and Korkie Analysis

MV optimization is a highly error-prone framework. Optimization inputs are always subject to estimation error. The fundamental source of the problem is that MV optimized portfolios are "estimation-error maximizers" (Michaud 1989a). MV optimization significantly over-weights (underweights) securities that have large (small) estimated returns, negative (positive) correlations, and small (large) variances. These securities are, of course, the ones most likely to have large estimation errors. The error maximization effect is the fundamental source of the unintuitive character of MV optimized portfolios. Essentially, the algorithm is too powerful for the level of information often available in investment data.

Portfolio optimization may often reduce performance even when forecast information is significant. Such results rationalize the behavior of many institutional investors, who have experienced the limitations of MV optimized portfolios firsthand and have voted with their feet by abandoning the procedure for other, less error-prone alternatives.

## The Statistical Character of Mean-Variance Efficiency

To enhance the value of MV optimization, it is necessary to understand the source of the instability and ambiguity identified by Jobson and Korkie. The key is to see that MV optimization is essentially a statistical procedure rather than one of computational technique. It is similar in many respects to constrained linear regression. Misunderstanding of the statistical nature of MV efficiency has led to many counterproductive or suboptimal investment practices. On the other hand, recognition of its statistical character can lead to procedures that may significantly improve its investment value.[10]

## Efficient Frontier Variance

An analysis of the statistical characteristics of MV efficiency may usefully begin with a description of the variability in the procedure.

---

[10] One of the earliest mentions of the efficient frontier as a sample statistic is in Roll (1979).

Consider the question: Does the efficient frontier have a variance? Initially, the question may appear frivolous: How can a curve have a variance? On reflection, however, the question is less obviously frivolous. An MV efficient frontier is a computation based on statistically estimated parameters. Consequently, it must have a variance. The question is how to estimate the variance.

Analytic solutions are available for the variance of the efficient frontier that include only linear constraints (Jobson 1991). In many situations of institutional interest, however, the optimization includes sign and other linear inequality constraints. In these cases, a variant of the Jobson and Korkie Monte Carlo simulation is the procedure of choice.

## The Statistical Equivalence Region

The idea for estimating the variance of an efficient frontier is to use the Jobson and Korkie resampling procedure to compute "statistically equivalent" efficient frontiers from the optimization inputs. The collection of resampled statistically equivalent efficient frontiers shows the variability implicit in efficient frontier estimation.

More specifically, for the efficient frontier in Exhibit 2.5, the data resampling simulation proceeds as follows:

1. Monte Carlo simulate 18 years of monthly returns based on the data in Tables 2.3 and 2.4 for the eight asset classes.

2. Compute optimization input parameters from the simulated return data.

3. Compute efficient frontier portfolios that satisfy the same constraints as those in Exhibit 2.5.[11]

4. Repeat steps 1–3 500 times.[12] By definition, each simulated efficient frontier is statistically equivalent to the efficient frontier in Exhibit 2.5.

5. To observe the variability in the efficient frontier estimation process, evaluate the mean and standard deviation of the simulated efficient frontier portfolios based on the optimization parameters in Tables 2.3 and 2.4.

---

[11] As described in chapter 2, this means computing 51 efficient portfolios, ranging from the minimum variance to the maximum expected return portfolios, satisfying base case constraint assumptions.

[12] Unless otherwise noted, all simulations that follow assume 500 efficient frontier replications.

**Exhibit 4.1:** Mean-Variance and Statistical Equivalence Region
Efficient Portfolios

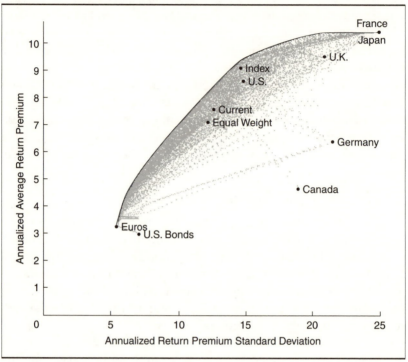

Exhibit 4.1 displays the original Exhibit 2.5 efficient frontier and
the 500 statistically equivalent resampled efficient frontier portfolios.
The area occupied by the simulated efficient frontier portfolios is the
MV efficient frontier "statistical equivalence" region.[13] The simulated
efficient frontier portfolios never plot above the original efficient frontier. If no variability existed, the simulated efficient frontiers would be
the same as Exhibit 2.5. To the extent that variability exists, the simulated efficient frontier portfolios vary from those in Exhibit 2.5 and plot
below the original efficient frontier.

Exhibit 4.1 dramatically illustrates the enormous, even startling,
variability implicit in efficient frontier portfolio estimation. Very wide
ranges of portfolios are statistically equivalent to the efficient frontier.
Indeed, it is unclear what reasonable portfolio is excludable from the

---

[13] The concept of the "statistical equivalence" region, discussed in Michaud (1989a), has
important antecedents in the work of Jobson and Korkie (1981). Also, see Jobson (1991)
and Jorion (1992).

set of statistically equivalent efficient portfolios.[14] The results highlight the importance of a statistical understanding of MV optimization.

Note that a simulated MV efficient frontier is not necessarily consistent with efficient frontier intuition and may not monotonically increase in expected return with increasing risk. For example, a given simulation may result in German equities having the highest average return. In this case, the simulated efficient frontier curves "down," toward the point representing German equity returns at the "upper" end of the simulated frontier.

The results have significant applications to investment practice. In particular, many investment organizations devote a great deal of time and effort tweaking optimization assumptions. The size of the statistical equivalence region in Exhibit 4.1 suggests that such practices may often have little investment merit or value.

## A Practical Investment Tool?

Faced with the level of variability inherent in MV portfolio optimization, should an investor abandon the technology? This is, in fact, a very reasonable conclusion.[15] MV optimization may often eliminate the investment value of information in return forecasts. In general, MV optimization requires modification and constraints (Frost and Savarino 1988).

In institutional practice, equity portfolio optimizations often have many constraints. In many sophisticated organizations, the constraints on equity portfolio structure are so extensive that they may all but define the "optimal" portfolio. Although such practices can be rationalized, given the limitations of traditional MV optimization, they cannot be recommended. In this context, optimizers provide little more than a computational convenience for structuring portfolios with little inherent investment content.

The statistical equivalence region vividly illustrates the instability and ambiguity of traditional MV optimization for investment management. However, the same results open the door to a fundamentally new perception of the statistical nature of MV efficiency. A number of statistical techniques may enhance MV optimization. This line of inquiry largely occupies the remainder of the text. The following chapters focus on seven approaches for enhancing MV optimization:

---

[14] In a related study, Chopra (1991) provides a simple three-asset example that illustrates how nearly optimal portfolios can be dramatically different in composition.

[15] See the comments in Jobson and Korkie (1981).

1. Statistical inference

2. The resampled efficient frontier

3. Portfolio efficiency analysis

4. Improved input estimation

5. Defining priors and benchmarks

6. Using forecasts rigorously

7. Avoiding common errors.

Each area can help to improve the investment value of optimized portfolios. Together they can have a substantial impact on the value of the optimization process. Properly managed, the outlook for MV optimization as a practical tool of investment management should be cautious optimism.

Chapter *5*

# Portfolio Review and Mean-Variance Efficiency

$M$any investors think of mean-variance (MV) efficiency as a tool for optimizing portfolios. However, not all portfolios need optimization. Some are close to the efficient frontier and are statistically indistinguishable from efficiency. A statistical test of portfolio MV efficiency may often be a convenient first step and a valuable alternative to MV optimization.

## Portfolio Review and Statistical Inference

In a portfolio review, an asset manager's role is to recommend optimal revisions. For some institutional managers, this function includes running the portfolio through an optimizer. As a first step, it may often be preferable to determine whether the portfolio needs revision. This may avoid the investment limitations of a portfolio optimization and eliminate unnecessary trading costs.

The question of whether a portfolio needs revision is one of statistical inference. A portfolio that is consistent with MV efficiency may not need revision. Alternatively, if the portfolio is inconsistent with efficiency, the portfolio may need revision and additional procedures may be required. Given the wide range of statistically equivalent portfolios shown in Exhibit 4.1, many diversified portfolios may not require revision.

## Tests of Asset Pricing Models

Statistical tests for the MV efficiency of a portfolio are available.[1] In general, these procedures test for the MV efficiency of "market" port-

---

[1] Jobson and Korkie (1982) and Shanken (1985) develop MV efficiency tests based on the F distribution. A recent review is given in Shanken (1996).

folios as an empirical test of asset pricing models.[2] Such tests have limited applicability for institutional equity management for two reasons. First, the tests allow short selling; sign-constrained MV efficiency often has significantly different characteristics.[3] Second, the test procedures compare the MV efficiency of a portfolio to the maximum Sharpe ratio portfolio.[4] However, the maximum Sharpe ratio portfolio is only one point on the efficient frontier and may not be most relevant in many cases of investment interest.[5] What is required is a test of MV efficiency for sign-constrained portfolios relative to relevant sign-constrained efficient portfolios.

## Heuristic Inference

The statistical equivalence region in Exhibit 4.1 populated by simulated sign-constrained efficient portfolios is a heuristic basis for MV efficiency inference. Referring to Table 2.2, consider inference for the MV efficiency of the current portfolio. The current portfolio plotted in Exhibit 4.1 is well within the statistical equivalence region. Consequently, the current portfolio appears consistent with MV efficiency and may not require optimization.

Although it is intuitively appealing, the procedure in the previous paragraph is not statistically rigorous. In particular, a statistical inference procedure requires control of type I error: the probability of rejecting the null hypothesis when it is true. The goal below is to transform the statistical equivalence region into a sample acceptance region so that it is useful for hypothesis testing.

## A Sample Acceptance Region

Assume a type I error of size $\alpha$. A $100(1 - \alpha)\%$ sample acceptance region for MV efficiency is an area under the efficient frontier that in-

---

[2] As pointed out by Roll (1977), the efficiency of the market portfolio is equivalent to the empirical validity of the capital asset pricing model (CAPM).

[3] When short selling is allowed, the efficient frontier is summarized by three "efficient set" parameters and the MV efficiency of a portfolio is determined solely by its Sharpe ratio, not its position in mean-variance space. The parameters are insufficient for describing the short-selling–constrained efficient frontier and are not useful for many practical applications.

[4] The maximum Sharpe ratio portfolio depends on the assumed return of a short-term riskless asset or the zero-beta portfolio. The zero-beta CAPM portfolio is developed in Black (1972).

[5] For example, an investor may be more interested in statistical equivalence with respect to the minimum variance portfolio than the maximum Sharpe ratio portfolio.

cludes, on average, $100(1 - \alpha)\%$ of resampled portfolios. The definition of an area under a curve from elementary calculus provides a simple method for approximating the sample acceptance region from the statistical equivalence region.[6] Divide the area under the efficient frontier into mutually exclusive column rectangles that include all the simulated portfolios.[7] Define the base of the rectangle as the minimum return point that contains $100(1 - \alpha)\%$ of the simulated portfolios in the rectangle. By construction, the curve connecting the midpoint of the base of the rectangles contains approximately $100(1 - \alpha)\%$ of the simulated portfolios under the curve. This curve is an estimate of the lower boundary of a $100(1 - \alpha)\%$ sample acceptance region. All portfolios on or below the efficient frontier and on or above the lower boundary are said to belong to the $100(1 - \alpha)\%$ acceptance region. As the number of efficient frontier portfolios, associated rectangles, and simulations increases, the approximation increases in accuracy.[8]

The area between the efficient frontier and the lower curve in Exhibit 5.1 is a Monte Carlo–estimated 90% sample acceptance region for the simulated statistically equivalent portfolios in Exhibit 4.1. The test for MV efficiency at the 90% acceptance level proceeds by determining whether the risk and return of a candidate portfolio is within the sample acceptance region. If the portfolio is within the sample acceptance region, no revisions may be required; if the candidate portfolio is outside the region, it probably requires revision.

Because of differences implied by sign-constrained portfolios, Jobson's (1991) analytic estimate of the sample acceptance region is substantially different in shape from the region in Exhibit 5.1. The differences are most dramatic near the maximum average return point of the sign-constrained efficient frontier. The area under the curve in

---

[6] The method used is called the Riemann integral in elementary calculus. The area under a curve is approximated with mutually exclusive rectangles that span the region. As the rectangles become dense, the approximation of the area under the curve becomes increasingly accurate.

[7] In this and the examples that follow, the end points defining the width of the fifty mutually exclusive rectangles that approximate the area under the curve are equal to the fifty adjacent pair efficient frontier portfolios.

[8] The astute reader may have noted that there is no fundamental reason why the rectangles that approximate the acceptance region need to be defined as column rectangles. They could as easily have been defined as row rectangles. Either procedure should result in approximately equivalent regions in most cases of practical interest. Differences between the two approaches are likely to be largely functions of inadequate approximations. As the approximations improve by increasing the number of efficient frontier portfolios and simulations, the results of the two approaches should be similar for many applications of interest.

**Exhibit 5.1:** Mean-Variance Efficient 90 Percent Sample Acceptance Region

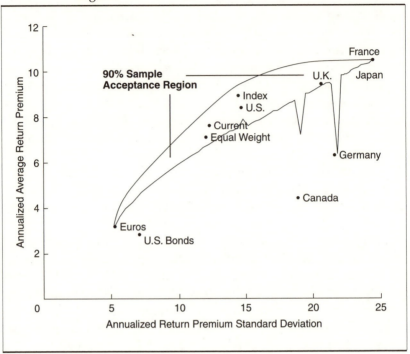

Jobson's acceptance region increases monotonically with risk, whereas the sign-constrained portfolio acceptance region in Exhibit 5.1 decreases near the maximum average return point.

Because the optimization in Exhibit 5.1 includes only eight assets, the sample acceptance region can have irregular properties. In this case, the sample acceptance region includes German equities and has a rather ragged lower-boundary. As the number of assets and simulations increases, the smoothness of the boundary of the acceptance region is likely to increase.[9]

The results in Exhibit 5.1 show that all three reference portfolios from Table 2.2 are well within the acceptance region and consistent with MV efficiency for a type I error of $\alpha = 0.10$. One important implication of statistical inference is a reduced need for portfolio turnover.

---

[9] The lack of smoothness of the boundary is also due to the particular number of approximating rectangles in the construction process, which, in this case, is a function of the number of computed efficient frontier portfolios.

In fact, many institutional portfolios may not need revision or may need fewer revisions with the use of statistical inference. Consequently, statistical inference may have important benefits for investment performance and the efficiency of capital investment.

## Statistical Inference for a Target Efficient Portfolio

Although it is useful as a first step, the sample acceptance region in Exhibit 5.1 has some significant investment management limitations. For example, according to Exhibit 5.1, the current portfolio is consistent with MV efficiency. However, is the portfolio statistically equivalent to every portfolio on the MV efficient frontier? If not, does it matter in practice? If a given portfolio is not statistically equivalent to an efficient portfolio that satisfies client risk objectives and constraints, it may still need revision. Statistical inference associated with a target efficient portfolio may increase the frequency of portfolio revisions relative to the test represented by Exhibit 5.1. Practical statistical inference may often require consideration of target efficient portfolios. In this case, statistical inference relative to a given efficient portfolio, rather than MV efficiency in general, may be of interest.

## Rank-Associated Efficient Portfolios

A first step to statistical inference with respect to an efficient frontier portfolio is to associate statistically equivalent efficient portfolios with each point on the MV efficient frontier. For example, the minimum-variance portfolio at the base of the efficient frontier in Exhibit 4.1 can be associated with the portfolios at the base of each simulated efficient frontier.[10]

Statistically equivalent efficient portfolios can also be associated with any other point on the efficient frontier. Recall that the efficient frontier and each statistically equivalent simulated efficient frontier in Exhibit 4.1 consists of 51 portfolios. Each efficient frontier portfolio is identifiable by its relative return rank. For example, the minimum variance portfolio has the lowest rank, or rank 1, relative to the 51 efficient portfolios in each efficient frontier. The maximum average return portfolio has the highest average return rank, or rank 51, in each efficient frontier. In similar fashion, any other portfolio on the efficient frontier

---

[10] This exercise is essentially the same as that in Jorion (1992).

**Exhibit 5.2:** Minimum Variance, Middle, and Maximum Average
Return Efficient Frontier Statistical Equivalent Portfolios

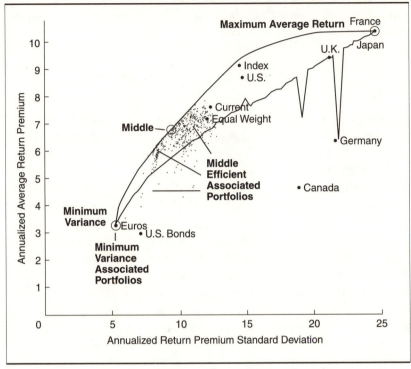

is associated with a relative return rank. Using this procedure, simulated efficient frontiers associate statistically equivalent portfolios with
efficient frontier portfolios in Exhibit 4.1. For future reference, define
the twenty-first efficient frontier portfolio in return rank as the
"middle" efficient frontier portfolio in Exhibit 4.1.[11]

Exhibit 5.2 displays the 500 rank-associated statistically equivalent
efficient portfolios from Exhibit 4.1 for three selected portfolios on the
efficient frontier: minimum variance, middle, and maximum average
return. The positions of the three MV efficient portfolios are indicated
by the circles on the efficient frontier. The exhibit shows that the rank-
associated simulated minimum variance portfolios cluster very tightly
at the base of the efficient frontier and cover a very small area under

---

[11] Subsequent discussions use this definition consistently. The ranking is from lowest to
highest average return. Note that the efficient frontier portfolios are not equally spaced
along the return spectrum at the high return end. Consequently, the twenty-first–rank
portfolio is slightly below the middle of the efficient frontier.

the curve. These portfolios are virtually indistinguishable from the base of the curve. At the other end of the efficient frontier, the rank-associated simulated maximum average return portfolios consist solely of asset classes and represent a disconnected set of points that is not identifiable with an area under the efficient frontier. The remaining scattered portfolios are rank-associated simulated middle efficient portfolios and represent a sparse area under the curve. The shape of the rank-associated regions varies in interesting ways depending on the position of the portfolio on the MV efficient frontier.

The rank-associated, statistically equivalent efficient portfolios have heuristic interest but limited value for identifying a region under the efficient frontier that is useful for statistical inference. Alternative methods of inference based on the rank-associated portfolios are discussed in chapters 6 and 7.

*Chapter* **6**

# Portfolio Analysis and the Resampled Efficient Frontier

*T*his chapter introduces new tools for portfolio analysis and revision. It also introduces an important new definition of portfolio efficiency, the "resampled efficient frontier," which may often be the criterion of choice for defining optimal portfolios in practice.

## Conceptual Portfolio Statistical Analysis

Suppose that statistical tests were available for the weights of efficient portfolios, similar to those for the coefficients in linear regression analysis.[1] Would they be useful for portfolio management? How would a manager use them?

The tests might identify the securities that contribute most significantly to portfolio efficiency. The tests might also identify the portfolio weights that deviate significantly from a target efficient portfolio. This information could be helpful in formulating a revision of the portfolio that enhances efficiency without recourse to optimization. The statistical procedures for portfolio analysis and revision discussed below have similar objectives and capabilities.

## Efficient Portfolio Statistical Analysis

The Monte Carlo efficient frontier simulations in chapter 5 are useful for analyzing the statistical characteristics of MV efficient frontier

---

[1] While constrained linear regression, suitably defined, may resemble MV optimization, there are many pitfalls when the variables are sign constrained (Geweke 1986).

portfolios. The information is implicit in the rank-associated simulated efficient portfolios illustrated in Exhibit 5.2. Compute the averages, standard errors, and t-statistics of the average of the portfolio weights of the rank-associated simulated efficient portfolios.[2] Define a "resampled efficient" portfolio as the average of the rank-associated simulated MV efficient portfolios.[3] Define the "resampled efficient frontier" as the collection of the resampled efficient portfolios associated with an MV efficient frontier.[4]

Tables 6.1–6.3 provide a statistical analysis of the minimum variance, middle, and maximum average return efficient frontier portfolios in Exhibit 5.2. The second column in each table displays the average asset weight of rank-associated simulated efficient portfolios or the resampled efficient portfolio for the indicated MV efficient portfolio. The third column shows the fifth-percentile value for the portfolio weight for the asset in the 500 simulations of efficient portfolios. The fourth column lists the ninety-fifth–percentile portfolio weight in the 500 simulations. The fifth column lists the standard error of the average portfolio weights in column 2. The sixth column displays the t-statistic of the average portfolio coefficient.[5] The seventh column displays the portfolio weights of the efficient portfolio. The table titles identify the efficient portfolio. The table footnotes provide the annualized mean and standard deviation of the return premium of the MV efficient portfolio (column 7) and the average (resampled efficient) portfolio (column 2).

The data in the tables represent a form of linear regression analysis of the MV efficient frontier portfolios. The range of coefficients within the fifth- and ninety-fifth–percentile bounds includes 90% of the simulated portfolio weights. Because the distribution of portfolio weights is not normal, the percentile bounds often provide a more useful and reliable understanding of statistical significance than the t-statistics.[6]

The data in Table 6.1 show that Euros dominate the structure of minimum variance portfolios; no other asset weight is statistically

---

[2] The procedure is analogous to that used in Fama and Macbeth (1973).

[3] Resampled efficiency may also be defined in terms of a quadratic "utility" function parameter. This alternative approach, discussed in the appendix, leads to similar results.

[4] The average of the simulated portfolio weights is a portfolio. The author and Robert Michaud jointly discovered and developed properties of the resampled efficient frontier set; patent pending.

[5] See Judge et al. (1988, 216–17), for a similar analysis.

[6] I am indebted to Philippe Jorion for this suggestion.

**Table 6.1:** Statistical Analysis: Minimum Variance Efficient Portfolio

| Asset Name | Resampled Efficient Portfolio | 5th Percentile | 95th Percentile | Standard Error | T-statistic | MV Efficient Portfolio |
|---|---|---|---|---|---|---|
| Canada | 0 | 0 | 0.01 | 0.01 | 0.30 | 0 |
| France | 0 | 0 | 0.01 | 0.00 | 0.23 | 0 |
| Germany | 0 | 0 | 0.01 | 0.00 | 0.35 | 0 |
| Japan | 0.02 | 0 | 0.04 | 0.01 | 1.09 | 0.01 |
| U.K. | 0 | 0 | 0.01 | 0.01 | 0.31 | 0 |
| U.S. | 0 | 0 | 0.01 | 0.00 | 0.21 | 0 |
| U.S. Bonds | 0 | 0 | 0 | 0.00 | — | 0 |
| Euros | 0.98 | 0.96 | 1 | 0.02 | 65.49 | 0.99 |

*Note:* MV efficient portfolio mean = 3.3%; standard deviation = 5.4%. Resampled efficient portfolio mean = 3.4%; standard deviation = 5.4%.

**Table 6.2:** Statistical Analysis: Middle Efficient Portfolio

| Asset Name | Resampled Efficient Portfolio | 5th Percentile | 95th Percentile | Standard Error | T-statistic | MV Efficient Portfolio |
|------------|-------------------------------|----------------|-----------------|----------------|-------------|------------------------|
| Canada | 0.01 | 0 | 0.07 | 0.04 | 0.23 | 0 |
| France | 0.08 | 0 | 0.32 | 0.11 | 0.69 | 0.05 |
| Germany | 0.03 | 0 | 0.20 | 0.07 | 0.45 | 0 |
| Japan | 0.13 | 0 | 0.42 | 0.13 | 1.03 | 0.15 |
| U.K. | 0.07 | 0 | 0.31 | 0.11 | 0.65 | 0.03 |
| U.S. | 0.22 | 0 | 0.43 | 0.16 | 1.37 | 0.32 |
| U.S. Bonds | 0.09 | 0 | 0.53 | 0.19 | 0.46 | 0 |
| Euros | 0.37 | 0 | 0.54 | 0.17 | 2.23 | 0.44 |

*Note:* MV efficient portfolio mean = 6.5%; standard deviation = 9.2%. Resampled efficient portfolio mean = 6.6%; standard deviation = 9.1%.

**Table 6.3:** Statistical Analysis: Maximum Average Return Efficient Portfolio

| Asset Name | Resampled Efficient Portfolio | 5th Percentile | 95th Percentile | Standard Error | T-statistic | MV Efficient Portfolio |
|---|---|---|---|---|---|---|
| Canada | 0.01 | 0 | 0 | 0.10 | 0.10 | 0 |
| France | 0.34 | 0 | 1 | 0.47 | 0.71 | 1 |
| Germany | 0.04 | 0 | 0 | 0.20 | 0.20 | 0 |
| Japan | 0.33 | 0 | 1 | 0.47 | 0.70 | 0 |
| U.K. | 0.16 | 0 | 1 | 0.37 | 0.44 | 0 |
| U.S. | 0.12 | 0 | 1 | 0.33 | 0.37 | 0 |
| U.S. Bonds | 0 | 0 | 0 | 0.05 | 0.05 | 0 |
| Euros | 0 | 0 | 0 | 0.00 | 0.04 | 0 |

*Note:* MV efficient portfolio mean = 9.9%; standard deviation = 17.3%. Resampled efficient portfolio mean = 10.5%; standard deviation = 24.4%.

significantly different from zero. The statistical results are consistent with the compact size of the area covered by the statistically equivalent portfolios at the base of the efficient frontier in Exhibit 5.2. The structure of the minimum variance efficient frontier portfolio is the most reliable of all portfolios on the efficient frontier. This should not be surprising because the minimum variance portfolio ignores the additional variability associated with optimizing expected portfolio return.

The results in Table 6.2 illustrate the wide level of variability of efficient portfolios over much of the MV efficient frontier. The largest resampled efficient portfolio weight for the middle efficient portfolio, Euros, is not significantly different from zero at the 5% level.[7] Note that the t-statistic for Euros is misleading in terms of asset weight statistical significance. All average portfolio coefficients are significantly different from one at the 5% level. The most important other components of the middle portfolio are Japanese and U.S. equities. The results are consistent with the wide dispersion of statistically equivalent portfolios displayed in Exhibit 5.2 for the middle portfolio. Note that the resampled efficient portfolio differs in some important instances from the middle MV efficient portfolio. As will be seen, this result is not anomalous.

The data in Table 6.3 present a strikingly interesting, perhaps unexpected, analysis of the maximum average return efficient frontier portfolio. Most notably, the MV efficient frontier portfolio differs substantially from the resampled efficient portfolio. These results are easy to rationalize. All simulated statistically equivalent maximum average return portfolios in Exhibit 5.2 consist of only one asset. Because of their nearly identical average return, Japan and France are nearly equally likely to be the simulated maximum average return efficient portfolio. Other simulations occasionally result in other indices as the maximum average return efficient asset. The average portfolio weights reflect the relative frequency of the asset having the highest simulated average return.[8] No average portfolio weight is statistically significantly different from zero. Although some average portfolio weights are statistically significantly different from 1 at the 5% level, four are not.

---

[7] According to the fifth-percentile lower bound, at least 5% of the resampled portfolio weights were zero. Some higher error rate than 5% is required to reject the hypothesis of insignificance.

[8] In this case, the weights of the average portfolio are interpretable as highest return binomial probabilities in a simulation.

**Exhibit 6.1:** Mean-Variance and Resampled Efficient Frontiers

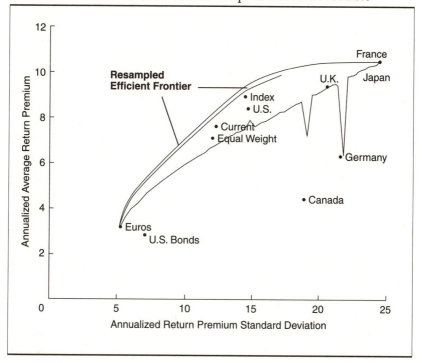

## The Resampled Efficient Frontier

Exhibit 6.1 displays the collection of all the resampled efficient portfolios associated with the MV efficient frontier in Exhibit 2.5. By definition, the resampled efficient frontier lies below and within the range of portfolio risk spanned by the MV efficient frontier. At the low-risk end, resampled efficient frontier portfolios are similar to their associated MV efficient portfolios. As portfolio risk increases, the similarities diminish.

The resampled efficient frontier is not simply a statistical artifact of portfolio simulation analysis but a computable and practical alternative investment strategy. The resampled efficient frontier portfolios are identifiable by resampling optimization inputs. The question of investment interest is whether the resampled efficient frontier provides a relevant and practical alternative for defining portfolio efficiency. The following discussion further explores this important issue.

## True and Estimated Optimization Inputs

Historic data, such as that in Tables 2.3 and 2.4, may not be useful for defining optimization inputs. This is because the data may not represent the true state of nature either during the historic period or for the investment horizon of interest. The basic problem is that the true optimization inputs are not only unknown but also unknowable. For any statistical procedure to be useful, the relevance of the input data for the forecast period is a key assumption. Given relevant data, the objective is to use the information optimally.

Assume that the historic data in Tables 2.3 and 2.4 define the true optimization inputs for a given investment horizon. Consequently, no other set of input assumptions is more appropriate as a basis for portfolio optimization. Although an MV efficient frontier portfolio is not necessarily the investment performance winner for a given draw of returns over the investment horizon, it is on average the best-performing portfolio for a given risk level. In this case, the resampled efficient frontier portfolios have little practical investment interest.

The problem with the scenario in the previous paragraph, and its conclusion, is that it is completely unrealistic and has little practical consequence. Optimization inputs, however estimated, contain estimation errors and are at best an informed guess of their true values. The more realistic situation is that the input data may be relevant but have estimation error.

What differentiates MV portfolio optimization from other applications of statistically estimated data is its tendency to overuse estimation errors. Exhibit 4.1 vividly illustrates that MV efficiency is very sensitive to estimation error, even assuming a stationary return process.[9] Resampled efficiency may help to address the issue of overfitting data that is endemic to MV efficiency.

## Testing Resampled Efficiency

Suitably modified, the Jobson and Korkie (1981) simulation method for measuring the impact of estimation error on the out-of-sample performance of MV efficient portfolios is applicable to sign-constrained MV optimization. With further modification, the basic

---

[9] The implicit assumption in simulation studies is that the return distribution reflected in the historic data is stationary for the investment horizon of interest. The nonstationarity of the return distribution adds another significant dimension of estimation error to MV optimization.

framework is also useful for measuring the out-of-sample relative performance of resampled efficiency.

Chapter 5 describes the rank-association process that relates sign-constrained MV efficient frontier portfolios with sign-constrained simulated efficient portfolios. The out-of-sample performance of the simulated efficient portfolios is measurable as the true Sharpe ratio, or reward-to-risk ratio. Average true Sharpe ratios for rank-associated sign-constrained simulated efficient portfolios play the same role as the average true Sharpe ratio in Jobson and Korkie's simulation of maximum Sharpe ratio portfolios.

In a Jobson and Korkie framework, the true optimization parameters, as represented by Tables 2.3 and 2.4, are unknowable. Each simulation is a possible out-of-sample realization of the true values of the optimization parameters. A resampled efficient frontier portfolio is the result of additional optimization input simulations based on each simulated set of optimization parameters. A test of resampled efficiency proceeds by comparing the true reward-to-risk ratios of rank-associated portfolios for each simulated MV efficient frontier relative to the same rank-associated portfolios that result from resampling the simulated efficient frontier parameters. The result is a single MV efficient portfolio and a single resampled efficient portfolio for each simulation and rank association.[10]

Table 6.4 summarizes the distribution of the reward-to-risk ratios for MV and resampled efficiency for the three portfolios in Tables 6.1–6.3.[11] The first row shows the mean of the true reward-to-risk ratios for the simulations of the three rank-associated portfolios for MV and resampled efficiency. The second and third rows provide the same information for the tenth and ninetieth percentiles of the reward-to-risk ratios. The fourth row displays the proportion of the simulations where resampled outperforms MV efficiency. The data reflect 500 simulated MV efficient frontiers estimated for 216 monthly periods. The resampled efficient frontier portfolios are defined from 500 simulations for each of the 500 simulated efficient frontiers.

The results in Table 6.4 show that, in nearly every instance, resampled efficiency is superior to MV efficiency. In particular, resampled efficiency is, on average, a uniformly superior investment

---

[10] See the appendix in this chapter for more details and results. I am indebted to Robert Michaud and Olivier Ledoit for critical assistance in defining the test framework.

[11] A more complete description of the distribution of reward-to-risk ratios is given in Table 6A.1 in the appendix in this chapter.

**Table 6.4:** Resampled Versus Mean-Variance Efficient Portfolios: True Reward-to-Risk Ratios

|                    | MV Efficiency | | | Resampled Efficiency | | |
|--------------------|---------|--------|---------|---------|--------|---------|
|                    | Minimum | Middle | Maximum | Minimum | Middle | Maximum |
| Mean               | 0.178   | 0.202  | 0.127   | 0.180   | 0.204  | 0.151   |
| 10th Percentile    | 0.172   | 0.188  | 0.125   | 0.175   | 0.194  | 0.134   |
| 90th Percentile    | 0.185   | 0.214  | 0.132   | 0.186   | 0.212  | 0.170   |
| Success Frequency  | —       | —      | —       | 0.976   | 0.590  | 0.984   |

**Exhibit 6.2:** Mean-Variance Versus Resampled Efficiency: True
Optimization Parameter Values

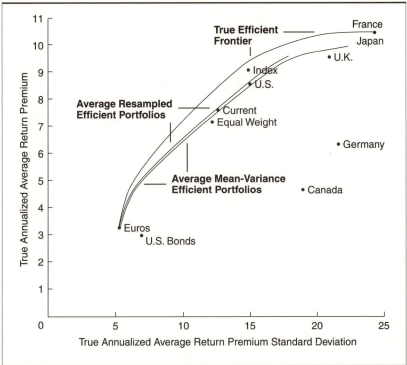

strategy that increases in importance as risk increases. Also, as shown
by the data in the bottom row, resampled efficiency is likely to be the
superior investment in practice.

Exhibit 6.2 provides a graphic illustration of the true average performance of portfolios defined by resampled and MV efficiency. Note
that the axes are defined as true return premium parameters. The top
curve is Exhibit 2.5, which, in this context, represents the true but unknowable optimization inputs in Tables 2.3 and 2.4. The lower curve is
the true average return and average risk of the 500 rank-associated
simulated MV efficient portfolios. The difference between the top and
bottom curves reflects the impact on average of estimation error for
sign-constrained efficient portfolios. The middle curve represents the
true average return and average risk of resampled efficient portfolios.
Consistent with Table 6.4, the exhibit shows that resampled efficient
portfolios are, on average, uniformly superior to MV efficiency. The
differences are relatively minimal at low risk levels but increase as risk

increases. Although it is not exact, a line parallel to the horizontal axis provides a reasonable approximation of rank association of portfolios on the two frontiers. Consequently, in rough terms, resampled efficiency on average reduces true risk relative to MV efficiency.[12] The results show that resampled efficiency has greatest impact on performance at high levels of risk. The test of resampled efficiency represented by Table 6.4, Exhibit 6.2, and the tables in the appendix to this chapter is conservative. Reducing the number of estimation periods and/or increasing the number of assets will increase the relative importance of resampled efficiency.

## Properties of Resampled Efficient Frontiers

To maximize expected return or reduce risk, MV efficient portfolios assume extreme asset weights. These extreme weights result in outlier portfolios that strongly depend on the values of a particular set of inputs. It is this outlier characteristic of MV portfolio efficiency that is the fundamental source of its limitations as a practical tool of investment management. Overreliance on the values of estimated parameters leads to instability, ambiguity, and likely poor out-of-sample performance.

Resampled efficiency deals directly with the fundamental limitations of MV optimization. Each resampled portfolio is a possible MV efficient portfolio associated with the original input data. By definition, the average resampled MV efficient portfolio is not an outlier. Resampled efficiency moderates the extreme portfolio weights associated with MV efficient portfolios.[13] Consequently, resampled efficient portfolios are less dependent on any particular set of optimization inputs. Less extreme portfolio weights are evident in the high–expected-return efficient portfolios but are also present to a lesser degree at the low-risk end of the efficient frontier. Because resampled efficient frontier portfolios are not outliers, they are more likely to provide safer and reliable investments in practice and better out-of-sample performance on average. Note also that portfolios with more moderate bets on assets may have additional practical investment benefits. These include

---

[12] See Table 6A.1 for further details.

[13] Moderation of extreme portfolio weights is a characteristic of admissible Stein estimators, discussed in chapter 8. In the case of the resampled frontier, the moderation of extreme portfolio weights may be subject to feasibility and the satisfaction of sign, budget, and other constraints. In the simple cases considered, a resampled efficient frontier portfolio may not moderate zero portfolio weights if a nonzero portfolio weight is infeasible.

reduced liquidity demands and likely lower trading costs in future portfolio rebalancings.

One of the most attractive features of resampled efficient portfolios is that they are often more reasonable investments and more consistent with investment intuition. To illustrate, the maximum average return MV efficient portfolio in Exhibit 6.1 represents a 100% bet on French equities. However, the optimization inputs for Japanese and French equities in Table 2.3 are virtually identical. Based purely on the historic data, many investors are likely to prefer an equal bet on both markets. In addition, the optimization inputs for U.K. and U.S. equities are not very different from Japanese and French equities. Consequently, the resampled efficient portfolio, consisting of bets on Japanese, French, U.S., and U.K. equities, may seem far more preferable than the 100% bet on French equities implied by MV efficiency.

Resampled efficient frontier portfolios deviate most significantly, and are likely to be most useful, at higher levels of portfolio risk, which is the region of the efficient frontier that is often of most interest to active managers. They may also be more effective in the context of better estimation procedures of optimization parameters.[14]

## Resampled Efficient Frontier Range

In Exhibit 6.1, the resampled efficient frontier spans roughly two-thirds of the range of portfolio risk as the MV efficient frontier. This smaller set of portfolio risk may appear to indicate a more limited range of useful investment opportunities for resampling efficient frontier investors. However, as Exhibit 6.2 shows, the reduced range of risk is simply an indication of the benefits of resampled efficiency. Resampled efficient portfolios may have less true risk with little, if any, reduction in true average return, relative to their rank-associated MV efficient portfolios. The likely reduction in risk is a reflection of the limitations of the reliability of the information in historic data for portfolio optimization, particularly at the high–expected-return end of the MV efficient frontier.

## Caveats

The investment attractiveness of resampled efficiency may be misinterpreted. The simulations do not prove that resampled efficient portfolios always perform better than MV optimized portfolios in practice.

---

[14] Chapter 8, which considers Stein estimation, discusses this topic further.

Resampled efficiency improvements in performance critically depend on the relevance of the inputs for the forecast horizon. If other inputs are more appropriate, the resampled efficient portfolios may perform less well than MV efficiency or an equal-weighted portfolio. The criterion does not obviate the need for better estimation methods or more appropriate optimization frameworks.

## Conclusion

Resampled efficiency is an important new tool for defining portfolio efficiency in practice. It is useful for understanding the statistical characteristics and practical limitations of MV efficiency. In addition, it may often enhance the out-of-sample investment value of optimized portfolios in the context of the MV efficiency criterion. Relative to MV efficiency, resampled efficient portfolios are likely to be more robust and investment intuitive, two useful characteristics in many institutional contexts.

## *Appendix*

# Resampled Efficiency Tests and Alternatives

*T*his appendix provides a more detailed presentation of the procedure and results for testing the out-of-sample performance of resampled versus MV efficiency. It also presents and compares an alternative approach to defining resampled efficiency based on parameters in quadratic utility optimization.

## Resampled Efficiency for Sign-Constrained Portfolios

In Jobson and Korkie (1981), a set of optimization inputs (e.g., Tables 2.3 and 2.4) are assumed to describe the true state of nature. Jobson and Korkie test the impact of estimation error on MV optimization by simulating optimization inputs and evaluating the performance of optimized portfolios with respect to the true value of the optimization parameters.

For MV optimization with only a budget constraint, the performance measure of choice is the average of the true reward-to-risk ratios of the simulated maximum Sharpe ratio portfolios.

For sign-constrained MV optimization, some method of associating each efficient frontier portfolio with a simulated efficient frontier portfolio is required. The associated rank method, described in chapter 5, associates sign-constrained efficient frontier portfolios of a given rank along the efficient frontier with the same rank simulated MV efficient frontier portfolios. The distribution of the true reward-to-risk ratios of similar rank simulated efficient portfolios provides a measure of the impact of estimation error on MV efficiency. In Table 6A.1, 500 simulations of MV efficient frontiers are performed, giving rise to 51 rank-associated portfolios in each simulation. In Exhibit 6.2, the bottom curve is the average return and average risk of the 500 simulated MV efficient portfolios for each rank-associated portfolio on the true efficient frontier.

Each of the 500 simulated MV efficient frontiers provides a candidate set of MV optimization parameters. An additional 500 simulations of each MV efficient frontier optimization inputs leads to a resampled efficient frontier portfolio for each rank-associated portfolio. The average of

**Table 6A.1A:** Rank-Associated True Reward-to-Risk Ratios: Mean-Variance Efficient Portfolios

|  | Minimum | Rank 11 | Middle | Rank 31 | Rank 40 | Rank 46 | Maximum |
|---|---|---|---|---|---|---|---|
| Minimum | 0.172 | 0.175 | 0.161 | 0.139 | 0.112 | 0.096 | 0.070 |
| 10th Percentile | 0.172 | 0.187 | 0.188 | 0.172 | 0.152 | 0.138 | 0.125 |
| Mean | 0.178 | 0.194 | 0.202 | 0.193 | 0.177 | 0.164 | 0.127 |
| Median | 0.178 | 0.195 | 0.204 | 0.195 | 0.180 | 0.164 | 0.125 |
| 90th Percentile | 0.185 | 0.201 | 0.214 | 0.212 | 0.198 | 0.188 | 0.132 |
| Maximum | 0.195 | 0.208 | 0.216 | 0.215 | 0.207 | 0.197 | 0.165 |
| Standard Deviation | 0.005 | 0.006 | 0.010 | 0.015 | 0.018 | 0.018 | 0.017 |
| Return (%) | 3.3 | 3.8 | 4.7 | 5.8 | 7.3 | 8.8 | 9.9 |
| Risk (%) | 5.4 | 5.6 | 6.7 | 8.6 | 12.0 | 15.8 | 22.7 |

**Table 6A.1B:** Rank-Associated True Reward-to-Risk Ratios: Resampled Efficient Portfolios

| | Minimum | Rank 11 | Middle | Rank 31 | Rank 40 | Rank 46 | Maximum |
|---|---|---|---|---|---|---|---|
| Minimum | 0.172 | 0.182 | 0.175 | 0.153 | 0.130 | 0.115 | 0.105 |
| 10th Percentile | 0.175 | 0.188 | 0.194 | 0.185 | 0.168 | 0.154 | 0.134 |
| Mean | 0.180 | 0.194 | 0.204 | 0.197 | 0.183 | 0.171 | 0.151 |
| Median | 0.179 | 0.195 | 0.205 | 0.198 | 0.184 | 0.171 | 0.151 |
| 90th Percentile | 0.186 | 0.199 | 0.212 | 0.210 | 0.199 | 0.188 | 0.170 |
| Maximum | 0.195 | 0.204 | 0.215 | 0.215 | 0.206 | 0.198 | 0.190 |
| Standard Deviation | 0.004 | 0.004 | 0.007 | 0.010 | 0.012 | 0.013 | 0.014 |
| Return (%) | 3.4 | 3.8 | 4.6 | 5.6 | 7.0 | 8.5 | 9.6 |
| Risk (%) | 5.4 | 5.6 | 6.5 | 8.1 | 11.1 | 14.5 | 18.5 |
| Success Frequency | 0.976 | 0.506 | 0.59 | 0.684 | 0.764 | 0.788 | 0.984 |

the 500 resampled efficient frontier portfolios for each MV simulated efficient frontier forms 500 resampled rank-associated efficient portfolios. The middle curve in Exhibit 6.2 is the average return and average risk of the 500 resampled efficient portfolios for each rank-associated portfolio on the true efficient frontier.

Table 6A.1 provides a more extensive description of the distribution of the true reward-to-risk ratio results in Table 6.4. There are two panels of data. The first is for MV efficiency and the second is for resampled efficiency. The additional information in Table 6A.1 relative to Table 6.4 includes

1. minimum, maximum, and median reward-to-risk ratios;
2. a more comprehensive set of rank-associated portfolios (11th, 31st, 40th, and 46th from a total of 51); and
3. average return and average risk of the resampled and MV efficient portfolios in the two bottom rows.

In particular, the data in the two bottom rows of Table 6A.1 are the basis of Exhibit 6.2 and evidence for the notion that, as a reasonable approximation, resampled efficiency on average reduces true risk relative to MV efficiency.

## Rank- versus λ-Associated Resampled Efficient Portfolios

One alternative approach for defining an association between efficient and simulated efficient frontier portfolios is to use a quadratic utility objective function. Given a value of λ (lambda), associate the efficient and simulated efficient sign-constrained portfolios that minimize:

$$\phi = \sigma^2 - \lambda^*\mu. \qquad (6\text{-}1)$$

Each value of λ defines a specific portfolio on the MV and simulated efficient frontiers. Varying λ from zero to infinity spans the set of efficient and simulated efficient frontier portfolios. Consequently, the average of λ-associated simulated efficient portfolios may be used to define a resampled efficient portfolio; varying λ from zero to infinity may serve as an alternative basis for defining the resampled efficient frontier.

Table 6A.2 on pages 68 and 69 displays the true reward-to-risk ratios for MV and resampled efficiency in the same test procedure and format as in Table 6A.1, where λ is used to associate simulated with efficient portfolios. The λ values are shown in the first row of Table 6A.2.

Lambdas and ranks play a similar role in defining portfolios along the efficient frontiers. Allowing for random variation and inexact correspondence, most of the corresponding results in Tables 6A.1 and 6A.2 appear roughly the same. However, as opposed to Table 6A.1, the results in Table 6A.2 indicate that λ association resampled efficiency may often increase true risk.[15] As a practical matter, the choice between the two approaches may simply be a matter of convenience. If substantive differences of interest exist, they await further research.

---

[15] For example, when λ equals 10, 15, and 20 in Table 6A.2, the average true risk is larger for resampled than for MV efficiency.

**Table 6A.2A:** λ-Associated True Reward-to-Risk Ratios: Mean-Variance Efficiency

|  | 0 | 10 | 15 | 20 | 50 | 100 | Infinity |
|---|---|---|---|---|---|---|---|
| Minimum | 0.172 | 0.169 | 0.152 | 0.137 | 0.089 | 0.085 | 0.070 |
| 10th Percentile | 0.172 | 0.188 | 0.186 | 0.179 | 0.147 | 0.125 | 0.125 |
| Mean | 0.178 | 0.201 | 0.200 | 0.195 | 0.170 | 0.152 | 0.127 |
| Median | 0.178 | 0.202 | 0.201 | 0.197 | 0.172 | 0.151 | 0.125 |
| 90th Percentile | 0.185 | 0.213 | 0.212 | 0.209 | 0.190 | 0.181 | 0.132 |
| Maximum | 0.195 | 0.216 | 0.216 | 0.217 | 0.215 | 0.204 | 0.165 |
| Standard Deviation | 0.005 | 0.009 | 0.011 | 0.013 | 0.018 | 0.021 | 0.017 |
| Return (%) | 3.3 | 4.4 | 5.0 | 5.5 | 8.1 | 9.3 | 9.9 |
| Risk (%) | 5.4 | 6.3 | 7.2 | 8.3 | 14.0 | 18.0 | 22.7 |

**Table 6A.2B:** $\lambda$-Associated True Reward-to-Risk Ratios: Resampled Efficiency

| | 0 | 10 | 15 | 20 | 50 | 100 | Infinity |
|---|---|---|---|---|---|---|---|
| Minimum | 0.172 | 0.174 | 0.160 | 0.147 | 0.110 | 0.102 | 0.105 |
| 10th Percentile | 0.175 | 0.192 | 0.189 | 0.182 | 0.155 | 0.143 | 0.134 |
| Mean | 0.180 | 0.202 | 0.200 | 0.196 | 0.173 | 0.161 | 0.151 |
| Median | 0.179 | 0.203 | 0.202 | 0.197 | 0.175 | 0.161 | 0.151 |
| 90th Percentile | 0.186 | 0.211 | 0.210 | 0.208 | 0.191 | 0.183 | 0.170 |
| Maximum | 0.195 | 0.216 | 0.215 | 0.215 | 0.207 | 0.200 | 0.190 |
| Standard Deviation | 0.004 | 0.008 | 0.009 | 0.011 | 0.015 | 0.016 | 0.014 |
| Return (%) | 3.4 | 4.5 | 5.1 | 5.8 | 8.1 | 9.0 | 9.6 |
| Risk (%) | 5.4 | 6.4 | 7.4 | 8.6 | 13.6 | 16.3 | 18.5 |
| Success Frequency | 0.976 | 0.678 | 0.538 | 0.490 | 0.714 | 0.840 | 0.984 |

*Chapter* **7**

# Portfolio Revision and Confidence Regions

*E*fficient frontier resampling provides an important window for understanding the fundamental statistical character of sign-constrained mean-variance (MV) optimization. As previously discussed, resampling methods may provide very useful information on the suitability of a portfolio for investment without optimization. In many cases, however, more specific information may be required. This chapter introduces some additional tools for portfolio inference and revision at the portfolio level and continues the exploration of the statistical characteristics of resampled efficiency.

## Confidence Intervals and Regions

The statistical analysis of the portfolios in Tables 6.1–6.3 has significant investment management limitations. Like linear regression analysis, the percentile statistics are useful primarily as a way of analyzing the importance of one asset while holding the other assets constant. It is often important, however, to determine whether the portfolio as a whole, rather than an asset weight, is consistent with efficiency. Such considerations require summaries of significance at the portfolio level.

Many readers are familiar with a confidence interval for a statistic. In elementary statistics, a $100(1 - \alpha)\%$ confidence interval is defined as an interval that, before sampling, contains the true value of the statistic of interest, such as the population mean, with probability $1 - \alpha$. Generally, confidence intervals summarize all the values of a statistic, such as the mean, that are consistent with the sample mean at type I error level $\alpha$. Confidence interval analysis is similar to the percentile statistic analysis shown in Tables 6.1–6.3.

A confidence region is a generalization of a confidence interval at the portfolio level. To discuss confidence regions, it is useful to think of a portfolio as a vector of portfolio weights. A vector is simply an ordered set of numbers representing the portfolio weight for each asset in the string. For example, Table 2.2 defines the current portfolio as an eight-dimensional vector of the portfolio weights 5, 10, 0, 20, 15, 20, 20, and 5. It is understood that the sixth element refers to the 20% portfolio weight for U.S. equities. In similar fashion, any other eight-dimensional vector with sum-to-100 nonnegative values may represent a portfolio of allocations to the eight asset classes in Table 2.2. Each simulated MV efficient frontier portfolio in Exhibit 5.1 represents an eight-dimensional random vector. The resampled efficient frontier represents sample means of these vectors.

## Resampled Efficiency and Distance Functions

In this chapter, the resampled efficient frontier defines the notion of portfolio efficiency. There are two reasons for focusing on resampled efficiency rather than MV efficiency. First, a resampled efficient portfolio is a sample mean vector. The statistical properties of the sample mean vector are often mathematically and statistically convenient. Second, resampled efficiency is likely to have the most practical investment interest.

The efficiency of a portfolio depends on whether the portfolio vector is "close" to the resampled efficient portfolio. Confidence regions require a notion of a distance function that compares the entire portfolio with a given resampled efficient portfolio.

Under standard assumptions, a sample mean vector has a well-known statistical distribution.[1] Although confidence region geometry is often complex, statistical inference and the definition of the confidence region are straightforward.[2] Statistical inference is associated with a test statistic that operates as a distance function. Unfortunately, the standard procedure for the sample mean vector is not valid for the resampled efficient frontier.[3]

---

[1] The usual assumptions include multivariate normal returns or sufficiently large random samples.

[2] See Appendix A in this chapter for a description of confidence regions and inference for the sample mean vector under standard assumptions.

[3] See Appendix A in this chapter.

# Resampled Efficient Frontier Confidence Regions

Two of the principal goals of resampling or bootstrap methods is to define test statistics and provide good estimates of confidence sets in situations where standard statistical methods may not be available or yield exact answers. For resampled portfolio efficiency, resampling statistical methods are useful and convenient.

Let $P$ be a vector of portfolio weights for any portfolio, and let $P_0$ be a vector of the portfolio weights of a given portfolio on the resampled efficient frontier. Let $S$ equal the covariance matrix of historic return premiums defined by Tables 2.3 and 2.4. The relative variance[4] or portfolio variance relative to $P_0$ is a natural basis to define a test statistic of the distance between portfolio $P$ and $P_0$. Define the confidence region resampling test statistic as

$$(P - P_0)' * S * (P - P_0) \leq \text{constant}^5 \qquad (7\text{-}1)$$

The simulation process provides a simple means of computing a constant that defines the test statistic in formula 7-1 and $100(1 - a)\%$ confidence region relative to $P_0$ on the resampled efficient frontier.[6] The distribution of the test statistic depends on the value of $P_0$. Table 7.1 provides estimates of the constant in formula 7-1 for the minimum variance, middle, and maximum average return resampled efficient portfolios in Exhibit 5.2. The constants reflect the range of values of relative variance that define the portfolios within a 90% confidence level resampled efficient region.

**Table 7.1:** Resampled Efficient Region: 90 Percent Confidence Level Test Statistics

|  | Minimum Variance | Middle | Maximum Average Return |
|---|---|---|---|
| Test Statistics | 0.028 | 3.0 | 20 |

---

[4] The relative variance for portfolio $P$ relative to $P_0$ is defined as $(P - P_0)' * S * (P - P_0)$.

[5] Formula 7-1 assumes vector and matrix operations. The term $P - P_0$ is the difference vector of portfolio weights. The term $(P - P_0)'$ is the transpose of the difference vector. $S$ is the historic return covariance matrix. The result of the matrix and vector products is a number.

[6] See Appendix B for further details.

**Exhibit 7.1:**  Resampled Minimum and Middle 90 Percent
Confidence Region

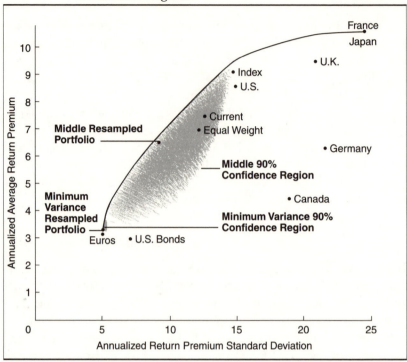

To illustrate the test, column 2 in Table 6.1 gives the portfolio
weights $P_0$ for the minimum variance resampled efficient portfolio. The
procedure is to substitute the portfolio vector for a given portfolio $P$ into
the formula 7-1 and compare the result to the value of the constant 0.028
in Table 7.1. If the relative variance or left-hand side of formula 7-1 is
less than the constant in Table 7.1, the portfolio is within the 90% confidence region. We can then infer that the portfolio is statistically equivalent to the resampled efficient portfolio at the 10% type I error level.[7]

It is of interest to visualize the range of portfolios that are statistically equivalent to portfolios on the resampled efficient frontier.[8] Ex-

---

[7] Note that the range of values of the relative variance for the maximum average return
resampled efficient portfolio is discrete. The percentile constant estimate in Table 7.1 is
less likely to be as accurate in this case. On the other hand, the information is the best
available.

[8] Another perspective on this visualization of the confidence regions is that they are
fuzzy sets for points on the resampled efficient frontier. Lower confidence levels may be
appropriate for some fuzzy set applications.

hibit 7.1 provides a description of the 90% confidence region for the minimum variance and middle resampled efficient portfolios.[9]

As Exhibit 7.1 shows, the risk level of the resampled efficient portfolio dramatically affects the shape of the confidence region. The confidence region for the minimum variance portfolio is very dense and compact. This result is consistent with the fact that minimum variance resampled efficiency is least ambiguous. The confidence region for the middle portfolio covers a much wider region of statistically equivalent portfolios and reflects much more ambiguity. The 90% confidence region for the maximum average return resampled efficient portfolio (not shown) covers almost the entire area under the efficient frontier. The ambiguity of maximum average return efficiency reflects the unreliability of the historic data at high levels of portfolio risk and requires additional tools.

## Simultaneous Confidence Intervals

Simultaneous confidence intervals are a relatively simple generalization of confidence intervals that provides some of the information of a confidence region in a convenient form for portfolio analysis.[10] As the name implies, simultaneous confidence intervals associate confidence intervals with each of the portfolio weights. The $100(1 - \alpha)$% simultaneous confidence intervals have the property that at least $100(1 - \alpha)$% of the simultaneously observed portfolio weights are within the bounds defined for each variable. This guarantees that any portfolio that is not within the simultaneous confidence region rejects the null hypothesis at type I error level $\alpha$. The computation of the simultaneous confidence intervals is straightforward and derives from the confidence regions plotted in Exhibit 7.1.[11]

Simultaneous confidence intervals often provide a simple way of rejecting consistency with resampled efficiency for many portfolios and of indicating portfolio revisions for inefficient portfolios—two of the primary objectives of the chapter. However, the simplicity of simultaneous

---

[9] The procedure is an exhaustive search algorithm, which can be very computationally intensive. Increments of all feasible portfolio weights define the search procedure. Plotting consists of all feasible portfolios that satisfy the range of relative variance, as defined by the constants in Table 7.1. The actual shape of the confidence regions is largely of pedagogic value.

[10] Simultaneous confidence interval procedures are described in Johnson and Wichern (1992, 191–202).

[11] Appendix B in this chapter provides a description of the procedure.

confidence intervals comes at the price of some significant limitations. One tradeoff is that the actual type I error level is likely to be significantly less than $\alpha$. This means that a portfolio that satisfies the simultaneous confidence intervals may still not be consistent with resampled efficiency for a given level of $\alpha$. Also, because the computation is based on the confidence regions in Exhibit 7.1, the estimation process may be computationally intensive.

## Examples of Simultaneous Confidence Intervals

Tables 7.2–7.4 provide estimates of the simultaneous 90% confidence intervals for the values of portfolio weights for the minimum variance, middle, and maximum average return resampled efficient frontier portfolios in Tables 6.1–6.3. Column 2 displays the lower bounds and column 4 displays the upper bounds for each asset for the indicated resampled efficient portfolio.

The results in Table 7.2 confirm the relatively specific character of minimum variance efficiency. Any portfolio that does not satisfy all the bounds of asset weights in Table 7.2 is inconsistent with minimum

**Table 7.2:** 90 Percent Simultaneous Confidence Intervals: Minimum Variance Resampled Efficient Portfolio

|  | Lower Bound | Resampled Efficient Portfolio | Upper Bound |
|---|---|---|---|
| Canada | 0 | 0 | 0.03 |
| France | 0 | 0 | 0.02 |
| Germany | 0 | 0 | 0.03 |
| Japan | 0 | 0.02 | 0.03 |
| U.K. | 0 | 0 | 0.03 |
| U.S. | 0 | 0 | 0.04 |
| U.S. Bonds | 0 | 0 | 0.19 |
| Euros | 0.78 | 0.98 | 1.00 |

*Note:* Accurate to within +/− 0.01 range.

variance resampled efficiency. Ninety percent of simulated minimum variance efficient portfolios require at least a 78% allocation to Euros. The upper bounds of the intervals indicate that only relatively minimal allocations in other assets are consistent with minimum variance resampled efficiency.

The results in Table 7.3 vividly illustrate the level of ambiguity that may exist for defining MV efficiency for more typical points on the resampled efficient frontier. The data rule out few reasonably diversified portfolios. For example, an equally weighted portfolio in Euros and Japanese and U.S. equities satisfies the bounds in the Table 7.3. The results are consistent with the wide dispersion of statistical equivalent portfolios displayed in the middle of Exhibit 7.1.

Table 7.4 shows that nearly any reasonable portfolio is within the 90% simultaneous confidence region for the maximum average return resampled portfolio. Efficient portfolio structure at high levels of risk is not very well defined. Note that estimation accuracy, which diminishes significantly in Tables 7.3 and 7.4 relative to Table 7.2, reflects the computationally intensive character of the procedure.

## Ambiguity and Portfolio Efficiency

Statistical analyses of efficient frontier portfolios provide a number of important insights into their investment value. In particular, the imprecision and ambiguity of portfolio efficiency becomes dramatically apparent.

MV optimization presents an illusion of precision that is seductive but generally fallacious and even dangerous. This illusion comes from the constrained linear regression character of MV optimization. MV optimization always finds some allocation of the assets that it considers optimal, without regard to statistical significance. However, the reliability of the allocations may be minimal or nonexistent even when large in relative terms. As in the case of the maximum average return efficient portfolio, the optimization is so ambiguous that an optimal solution may not be statistically distinguishable from almost any reasonable alternative. As the analyses indicate, only low-risk efficient portfolios provide relatively unambiguous allocations for this data set.

The imprecision of portfolio efficiency highlights the importance of the statistical analysis of MV optimized portfolios. In econometrics, statistical analysis of linear regressions is standard operating procedure. Such analyses also need to be an integral part of portfolio optimization if it is to become a useful and effective investment tool.

**Table 7.3:** 90 Percent Simultaneous Confidence Intervals: Middle Resampled Efficient Portfolio

|  | Lower Bound | Average Coefficient | Upper Bound |
|---|---|---|---|
| Canada | 0 | 0.01 | 0.42 |
| France | 0 | 0.07 | 0.35 |
| Germany | 0 | 0.03 | 0.35 |
| Japan | 0 | 0.14 | 0.35 |
| U.K. | 0 | 0.08 | 0.42 |
| U.S. | 0 | 0.22 | 0.70 |
| U.S. Bonds | 0 | 0.09 | 0.84 |
| Euros | 0.02 | 0.37 | 0.86 |

*Note:* Accurate to within +/− 0.07 range.

**Table 7.4:** 90 Percent Simultaneous Confidence Intervals: Maximum Average Return Resampled Efficient Portfolio

|  | Lower Bound | Average Coefficient | Upper Bound |
|---|---|---|---|
| Canada | 0 | 0.01 | 0.81 |
| France | 0 | 0.34 | 1.0 |
| Germany | 0 | 0.04 | 0.9 |
| Japan | 0 | 0.33 | 1.0 |
| U.K. | 0 | 0.16 | 1.0 |
| U.S. | 0 | 0.12 | 1.0 |
| U.S. Bonds | 0 | 0.00 | 0.9 |
| Euros | 0 | 0.00 | 0.91 |

*Note:* Accurate to within +/− 0.09 range.

Unfortunately, the result of a statistical analysis of portfolio efficiency may often be to show how little reliable investment information is available. At a minimum, knowing that little is certain is better than the illusion of certainty that currently pervades the perception of portfolio optimization. One reliable lesson is that managers should seldom take portfolio optimizations literally and should often feel free to include valid judgment in the portfolio management process.[12] These results also serve to motivate the importance of employing more powerful tools for defining portfolio efficiency.

## Practical Considerations

The two methods of portfolio revision analysis discussed in this chapter—confidence region testing and simultaneous confidence intervals—have very different practical considerations and tradeoffs.

The computational intensity of the confidence region procedure is relatively minimal, especially when compared to simultaneous confidence intervals. In particular, the algorithms used in the text for computing simultaneous confidence intervals are unlikely to be practical in many cases. Various attempts at speeding up the search algorithm were not successful.

From a perspective of ease of analysis, the simultaneous confidence intervals are more convenient than the confidence region test in formula 7-1. This is because the simultaneous confidence tables summarize all the necessary information for testing any candidate portfolio. In contrast, the more exact confidence region procedure requires the computation of the test statistic for each portfolio of interest.

---

[12] Chapter 11 rigorously addresses this issue.

## *Appendix A*

# Confidence Region for the Sample Mean Vector

$T$he computation of a confidence region for a sample mean vector often assumes a random sample of vectors from a multivariate normal distribution (Johnson and Wichern 1992, chapter 5). In this case, the sample mean vector has an $F$ distribution with $p$ and $n - p$ degrees of freedom, where $p$ denotes the rank of the covariance matrix and $n$ the number of random samples. If the sample size is large enough, the distribution is approximately multivariate normal and the $F$ distribution is applicable. The test statistic for the vector of the sample mean is as follows:

$$(\bar{x} - \mu_0)' * C^{-1} * (\bar{x} - \mu_0) \leq \text{constant} \qquad (7A\text{-}1)$$

Here, $\bar{x}$ is the sample mean vector of the random vectors and $C$ is the sample covariance matrix of random vectors. The distribution of the statistic in formula 7A-1 is an $F$ distribution dependent on the number of observations and degrees of freedom or rank of the positive definite covariance matrix. The formula 7A-1 is interpretable as a normalized distance function of the sample mean vector. The simultaneous confidence interval is the collection of vectors that satisfy formula 7A-1.

The confidence region centered at the resampled efficient portfolio is, in general, the area contained in a tilted ellipse, where the tilt depends on the correlation of return between the two assets. For portfolios with three or more assets, the values of the portfolio weights that lie in a resampled efficient frontier confidence region has an $N$-dimensional ellipsoid geometry that is often hard to visualize.

For the resampled efficient frontier, the portfolio weights from the resampling of MV efficient portfolios define the sample mean vector and covariance matrix. The budget constraint reduces the rank of the covariance matrix by 1. For sign-constrained efficient portfolios, additional issues arise. For example, the sign constraint leads to a minimum variance resampled portfolio in Table 6.1 that depends largely on the return of one asset. In this case, sign constraints may significantly reduce the rank of the portfolio covariance matrix. Consequently, the assumptions of the test statistic of formula 7A-1, as applied to resampled MV efficient frontier portfolios, is invalid.

*Appendix B*

# Computing Confidence Regions and Simultaneous Intervals

The  test statistic in formula 7-1 provides a formula for inference and confidence region estimation for resampled efficient frontier portfolios. Portfolio variance is based on the covariance return matrix. The relative variance is the variance of a portfolio relative to another. In formula 7-1, the relative variance is defined with respect to a resampled efficient frontier portfolio.

To compute the test statistic constants in Table 7.1, the relative variance of a resampled efficient frontier portfolio is estimated from the 500 simulations of the rank-associated resampled MV efficient frontier portfolios. The constant is the percentile value of sorted estimates of the relative variance in formula 7-1 of the 500 resampled MV efficient portfolios. For example, the constants in Table 7.1 come from the ninetieth percentile value of the relative variance from the 500 simulated efficient frontier portfolios in Exhibit 5.2.

Simultaneous confidence intervals follow from computing the confidence regions in Exhibit 7.1. The procedure is to compute the maximum and minimum portfolio weight for each asset for all portfolios within the confidence region for a given confidence level. Any portfolio outside the simultaneous confidence interval bounds is not consistent with resampled efficiency at the indicated confidence level. The computation depends on the search algorithm for finding the confidence region portfolios in Exhibit 7.1. To be valid, the results must reflect a comprehensive search of all feasible portfolios that satisfy the test statistic of formula 7-1 for a given resampled efficient portfolio. The results in Tables 7.2–7.4 used an exhaustive search algorithm to ensure validity and reasonable accuracy. Simultaneous confidence intervals in practice require development of more computationally efficient algorithms for many cases of practical interest.

*Chapter* **8**

# Input Estimation
# and Stein Estimators

$T$he investment value of optimized portfolios depends on proper input estimation. For many analysts and investors, input estimation methods may seem uncontroversial and hardly worth extended discussion. For example, for asset allocation studies, the sample means, standard deviations, and correlations of historic returns seem obvious and reliable input estimates.[1] However, many common estimation methods are suboptimal and are one of the most important causes of the limitations of mean-variance (MV) optimization in practice. In some important instances, better methods have been available to the investment community for many years. The reason that better procedures are unused is probably that the seriousness of the limitations of traditional estimation methods and their investment implications are not understood.[2]

Intuition is unreliable because portfolio optimization requires multivariate estimation; that is, the simultaneous estimation of means, standard deviations, and correlations. For related assets, there is likely to be information in the group of returns that can improve parameter estimates for each variable. "Stein" estimators use group information to improve estimation.[3] These methods, properly used, may lead to dramatically different and more intuitive optimized portfolios.

---

[1] Stock portfolio optimization typically uses sophisticated multivariate statistical methods for input estimation. Risk models, which use linear regression or factor analysis techniques, supplant simple covariance estimation in many cases. Equity return estimation may also use many advanced statistical methodologies. The topics of the chapter, admissibility and Stein estimators, are of interest for estimating optimization inputs in any context.

[2] Important exceptions are Jobson, Korkie, and Ratti (1979, 1980) and Jobson and Korkie (1981), who use James-Stein (1961) estimation to improve MV optimization.

[3] Named after Charles Stein, a pioneer of modern multivariate statistical estimation.

This chapter presents some basic principles of multivariate estimation and introduces four Stein estimators for MV optimization. It also addresses some limitations of ad hoc methods for estimating risk in equity portfolio optimization. Stein estimation also provides a framework for an additional test of the performance of resampled versus MV efficiency.

## Admissible Estimators

A statistic is admissible if no other is always better.[4] Intuitively, admissibility is a minimal condition for using a statistic. The reader may wonder why anyone uses a statistic that is not admissible. However, the investment community persists in using many inadmissible statistics.

Charles Stein (1955) astonished the scientific community by showing that sample means are not an admissible statistic for a multivariate population mean under very general conditions. Stein's result implies that there are uniformly better methods for estimating optimization means than the sample mean in many cases.

It is hard to understand why many financial economists and investment practitioners have ignored for so long methods that have the potential to significantly improve the investment value of optimized portfolios. This is especially true because simple and useful Stein methods appropriate for portfolio optimization have been available for at least 35 years.[5] Interestingly, financial economists and investment practitioners are not alone.[6]

## Bayesian Procedures and Priors

Stein estimators are generally examples of Bayesian statistical procedures. Bayesian procedures assume a prior. A prior is either a reasonable guess at the answer or an assumption that imposes exogenous structure on potential solutions. Bayesian methods transform the optimization by reducing dependence on pure statistically estimated data. Many of the most powerful methods in modern statistics are Bayesian.

---

[4] More precisely, an estimator is admissible if no other estimator is uniformly better for a given loss function.

[5] For example, James and Stein (1961).

[6] See Efron and Morris (1975) and Copas (1983) for discussions of some of the Stein estimator controversy.

Bayesian procedures are the basis of many of the proposed techniques for improving MV optimization.

Bayesian priors for parameter estimates and efficient portfolios arise naturally in many investment contexts. The assumption that all assets have the same mean is a simple Bayesian prior for optimization parameters. The assumed efficiency of an investable index is a common portfolio prior.

The development of admissible Stein estimators for optimization input estimation is an area of ongoing research. When used appropriately, Stein methods may significantly increase the investment value of optimization technology. Development of appropriate priors is an important issue in many applications. Chapters 9 and 10 discuss applications of Bayesian portfolio priors. In this chapter, the focus is on applications of Stein estimation and Bayesian parameter priors.

## Four Stein Estimators

Stein estimators are typically "shrinkage" operators. The amount of shrinkage may depend on the consistency of the prior with sample data. For example, suppose the prior for the means of $N$ assets is the global mean. A Stein estimator of the means may shrink sample means more toward the global mean if they are dissimilar than if they are not. The prior provides an anchor to the estimation process that tends to reduce estimation ambiguity and optimization instability while increasing investment relevance.

A number of Stein estimators are available for MV optimization estimation.[7] These include the James-Stein (1961), Frost-Savarino (1986), Ledoit (1994, 1997), and Stein (1982) estimators. The James-Stein procedure is an estimator for portfolio means. The Frost-Savarino procedure is a joint estimator of the means and covariances. The Ledoit and Stein procedures are estimators for the covariance matrix.

## James-Stein Estimator

The James-Stein estimator for the means is the most widely known Stein estimator.[8] Because the formula is so widely applicable, it may be

---

[7] Some early applications to MV optimization include Jorion (1986) and Brown (1976).

[8] There are some closely related versions. The one that may be most useful for MV optimization is the positive rule empirical James-Stein estimator that allows for unequal variances and assumes a global equal mean prior (Efron and Morris 1977, 123).

useful to discuss the formula in some detail. The formula for the Stein estimator of the mean of asset $i$, $\hat{\mu}_i$, is:

$$\hat{\mu}_i = \bar{x} + c_i(\bar{x}_i - \bar{x}) \tag{8-1}$$

where $\bar{x}$ = global sample mean, $\bar{x}_i$ = sample mean of asset $i$, $c \geq 0$.[9] This estimator shrinks the sample mean $\bar{x}_i$ to the global mean $\bar{x}$, depending on asset variance $\sigma_i^2$. Shrinkage increases as a function of distance from the global mean and asset variability.[10]

The James-Stein estimator for the mean may often have a significant effect on optimization inputs and results. Consider the return premium data in Table 2.3. The monthly global mean is 0.59% (7.0% annualized). Many of the equity assets deviate significantly from the global mean and have large standard deviations. Consequently, they are candidates for significant shrinkage. On the other hand, although bond assets have an average return that also deviates substantially from the global mean, the level of variability is less and shrinkage to the global mean likely to be less.

Table 8.1 displays the James-Stein estimates of monthly average return premiums corresponding to Table 2.3. For convenience, Table 8.1 also reproduces the monthly standard deviations. Note that five of the six equity average returns shrank to the global mean.[11]

The James-Stein procedure highlights the substantial volatility and ambiguity implicit in the data in Table 2.3. The estimator radically alters the perceived information in the historic data and conveys interesting investment implications. One interpretation is that, given the level of variability, the relatively large average returns of many equity asset classes may be unreliable forecasts of future performance.

## James-Stein Mean-Variance Efficiency

Exhibit 8.1 displays the efficient frontier that results from replacing the historic sample means with the James-Stein estimates in Table 8.1. Exhibit 8.1 also displays the resampled efficient frontier and the 90% acceptance region based on procedures defined in chapters 5 and 6. Tables

---

[9] $c_i = \max\{0, 1 - (k-3)\,\sigma_i^2/(\Sigma(\bar{x}_i - \bar{x})^2)\}$, where $k$ = number of assets, $k \geq 3$, $\sigma_i^2$ asset $i$ variance.

[10] See also Efron and Morris (1973).

[11] One alternative is to shrink the equity assets separately from the bond assets because the level of variability is so different. However, in this case, the James-Stein estimator leads to shrinkage to the global mean for all equity assets. The Table 8.1 results seem preferable from a number of perspectives.

**Table 8.1:** Monthly Dollars (Net) James-Stein Returns (Percentages), January 1978–December 1995

|  | Mean | Standard Deviation |
|---|---|---|
| Canada | 0.59 | 5.47 |
| France | 0.59 | 7.00 |
| Germany | 0.59 | 6.19 |
| Japan | 0.59 | 7.01 |
| U.K. | 0.59 | 5.99 |
| U.S. | 0.60 | 4.28 |
| U.S. Bonds | 0.31 | 1.99 |
| Euros | 0.30 | 1.52 |

8.2–8.5 provide statistical analyses of the middle and maximum average return portfolios, similar to Tables 6.2, 6.3, 7.3, and 7.4. Because the James-Stein estimator changes only the return estimates, the minimum variance portfolio in Exhibit 8.1 is the same as in Tables 6.1 and 7.2.

Exhibit 8.1 shows that the empirical James-Stein estimator may lead to very different optimal asset allocations than that of classic MV efficiency analysis. Although not statistically significant in most cases, the efficient frontier results shown in Tables 6.1, 8.2, and 8.4 indicate that (1) U.S. equities dominate at high risk, (2) U.S. equities and bonds and Euros dominate at intermediate risk, and (3) Euros dominate at low risk.

Note that the current portfolio is no longer in the 90% acceptance region.[12] Accordingly, the test suggests revising the current portfolio before investment. Comparing this result to Exhibit 5.1 indicates that

---

[12] In this case, horizontal rectangles that span the return axis, rather than vertical rectangles that span the risk axis, may more properly estimate the sample acceptance region. This is because the James-Stein estimated risk of many equity assets is not within the range of values of efficient risk portfolios and does not get included in the estimation of the sample acceptance region. The current portfolio remains outside the sample acceptance region independent of which method of computing the sample acceptance region is used.

**Exhibit 8.1:** James-Stein Mean-Variance Efficient Frontier, Resampled
Frontier, and 90 Percent Acceptance Region

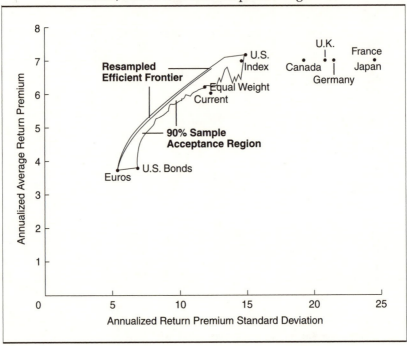

the reduction of statistical noise in the MV optimization process due to
James-Stein estimation provides a finer resolution of the notion of in-
vestment-acceptable portfolios.

Tables 8.3 and 8.5 display the simultaneous 90% confidence intervals for the middle and maximum average return efficient frontier
portfolios. The results in Table 8.3 rule out few reasonably diversified
portfolios as inefficient. For example, an equally weighted portfolio of
all eight assets is consistent with efficiency. Given the range of error in
the estimation process, the data in Table 8.5 for the maximum average
return portfolio hardly rule out the efficiency of any feasible portfolio.
These results reinforce the perception of the ambiguity of portfolio efficiency for high-return portfolios.

The results in Exhibit 8.1 show that the James-Stein resampled
frontier is very close to the efficient frontier over much of its range. The
reward-to-risk ratios for the resampled efficient frontier are close to
those of the MV efficient frontier and are often no lower. The pro-
nounced differences occur at the high-return end. Another notable dif-

**Table 8.2:** Statistical Analysis: James-Stein Middle Efficient Portfolio

| Asset | Resampled Efficient Portfolio | 5th Percentile | 95th Percentile | Standard Error | T-statistic | MV Efficient Portfolio |
|---|---|---|---|---|---|---|
| Canada | 0.04 | 0 | 0.19 | 0.08 | 0.45 | 0 |
| France | 0 | 0 | 0.02 | 0.01 | 0.27 | 0 |
| Germany | 0.05 | 0 | 0.16 | 0.06 | 0.77 | 0.07 |
| Japan | 0.06 | 0 | 0.13 | 0.05 | 1.17 | 0.08 |
| U.K. | 0.01 | 0 | 0.07 | 0.04 | 0.31 | 0 |
| U.S. | 0.19 | 0 | 0.43 | 0.14 | 1.33 | 0.32 |
| U.S. Bonds | 0.30 | 0 | 0.74 | 0.3 | 1.0 | 0 |
| Euros | 0.35 | 0 | 0.97 | 0.27 | 1.28 | 0.53 |

*Note:* MV efficient portfolio mean = 5.31%; standard deviation = 8.01%. Resampled efficient portfolio mean = 4.88%; standard deviation = 7.25%.

**Table 8.3:** 90 Percent Simultaneous Confidence Intervals: James-Stein Middle Efficient Portfolio

|  | Lower Bound | Resampled Efficient Portfolio | Upper Bound |
|---|---|---|---|
| Canada | 0 | 0.03 | 0.32 |
| France | 0 | 0 | 0.16 |
| Germany | 0 | 0.05 | 0.24 |
| Japan | 0 | 0.06 | 0.24 |
| U.K. | 0 | 0.02 | 0.24 |
| U.S. | 0 | 0.19 | 0.48 |
| U.S. Bonds | 0 | 0.31 | 0.88 |
| Euros | 0.04 | 0.34 | 1.00 |

*Note:* Accurate to within +/− 0.08 range.

ference is that the range of portfolio risk of the resampled frontier is significantly restricted.

Comparing the results in Tables 6.2 and 6.3 with those in Tables 8.2 and 8.4 shows that both Stein estimation and the resampled efficient frontier tend to moderate the extreme bets associated with MV optimized portfolios. However, James-Stein MV efficient portfolios still have extreme bets relative to their corresponding resampled frontier portfolios (see Tables 8.2 and 8.4). James-Stein estimation moderates, but does not eliminate, the tendency of MV efficiency to create extreme portfolios. The outlier characteristics of MV efficient portfolios are most significant at high expected return, where the resampled and MV efficient frontiers have the greatest deviation. Although the James-Stein estimator may be superior for estimating asset means in many cases, the results provide an unfamiliar perspective on historic data that is likely to require many investment practitioners to significantly adjust their investment intuition.

## James-Stein Estimator Test of Resampled and Mean-Variance Efficiency

By definition, the James-Stein estimates of the optimization input parameters are likely to be closer to the true population values than

**Table 8.4:** Statistical Analysis: James-Stein Maximum Average Return Efficient Portfolio

| Asset | Resampled Efficient Portfolio | 5th Percentile | 95th Percentile | Standard Error | T-statistic | MV Efficient Portfolio |
|---|---|---|---|---|---|---|
| Canada | 0.19 | 0 | 1 | 0.36 | 0.52 | 0 |
| France | 0.04 | 0 | 0.02 | 0.19 | 0.2 | 0 |
| Germany | 0.1 | 0 | 1 | 0.24 | 0.43 | 0 |
| Japan | 0.06 | 0 | 0.23 | 0.16 | 0.38 | 0 |
| U.K. | 0.05 | 0 | 0.17 | 0.2 | 0.25 | 0 |
| U.S. | 0.45 | 0 | 1 | 0.46 | 0.98 | 1 |
| U.S. Bonds | 0.06 | 0 | 1 | 0.24 | 0.26 | 0 |
| Euros | 0.05 | 0 | 1 | 0.23 | 0.24 | 0 |

*Note:* MV efficient portfolio mean = 7.25%, standard deviation = 14.89%. Resampled efficient portfolio mean = 6.73%, standard deviation =12.61%.

**Table 8.5:** 90 Percent Simultaneous Confidence Intervals: James-Stein
Maximum Average Return Efficient Portfolio

|  | Lower Bound | Resampled Efficient Portfolio | Upper Bound |
|---|---|---|---|
| Canada | 0 | 0.18 | 0.90 |
| France | 0 | 0.04 | 0.90 |
| Germany | 0 | 0.10 | 0.90 |
| Japan | 0 | 0.06 | 0.80 |
| U.K. | 0 | 0.05 | 1.0 |
| U.S. | 0 | 0.45 | 1.0 |
| U.S. Bonds | 0 | 0.06 | 1.0 |
| Euros | 0 | 0.05 | 1.0 |

*Note:* Accurate to within +/− 0.1 range.

the Table 2.3 historic data. This observation suggests a test of the out-
of-sample investment value of resampled compared to MV efficient
frontiers.[13]

Assume that the true underlying optimization inputs are well approximated by the data in Tables 8.1 and 2.4. Compare the resampled
performance of the middle and maximum average return portfolios on
the MV and resampled efficient frontiers as defined in Tables 6.2 and
6.3. The MV and resampled efficient portfolios compete in a James-
Stein estimated investment environment. The simulations are otherwise as defined in Exhibit 4.1. The data in Table 8.6 summarizes the
results of 100,000 simulations. Table 8.6 shows that resampled efficient
portfolios have higher average return than their rank-associated MV
efficient portfolios. Note that the maximum average return resampled
efficient portfolio also had much less risk. These results are consistent
with the hypothesis that resampled efficient portfolios are more likely
to outperform out of sample relative to MV efficient portfolios. The results indicate that resampled efficient frontiers are more robust and

---

[13] Suggested by Robert Michaud.

**Table 8.6:** Mean-Variance (MV) versus Resampled Efficient Returns (Annual Percentages): James-Stein Inputs

|  | Middle MV Efficient | Middle Resampled | Maximum MV Efficient | Maximum Resampled |
|---|---|---|---|---|
| Mean | 5.67 | 5.74 | 6.78 | 6.80 |
| Standard Deviation | 9.0 | 9.4 | 24.3 | 17.1 |
| Median | 5.66 | 5.73 | 6.85 | 6.59 |

likely to improve investment performance even when the true optimization inputs differ from those used in their definition.

It is interesting to note the inverse relationship between risk and median performance in the simulations. Although the middle MV efficient portfolio had less variability and larger median return, the maximum MV efficient portfolio had more risk and less median return relative to the resampled efficient portfolios.

## Frost-Savarino Estimator

The Frost and Savarino (1986) Stein estimator is one of the most interesting proposed for MV optimization. Notably, it is a joint estimator of the means and covariances. The prior is the efficiency of an equal-weighted portfolio.

Exhibit 8.2 illustrates the Frost-Savarino efficient frontier for the data in Exhibit 2.5. Comparing these results to Exhibit 2.5, note that the Frost-Savarino frontier shifts downward and slightly inward at the high-return end and upward and slightly inward at the low-return end. Essentially, the Frost-Savarino frontier shrinks toward the equal-weighted portfolio. The procedure generally has less impact on MV optimization inputs than the James-Stein estimator.

Frost-Savarino Stein estimation has some attractive properties. It is the only procedure that estimates all the MV optimization parameters in a unified framework, an approach that seems most appropriate for portfolio optimization. It is a less severe adjustment of optimization inputs than James-Stein. On the other hand, the procedure has significant limitations. The prior assumes that all means, variances, and cor-

**Exhibit 8.2:** Frost-Savarino Efficient Frontier

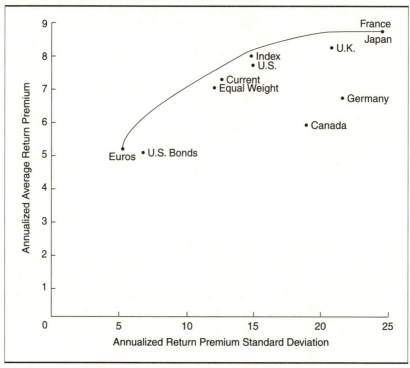

relations are the same. It is therefore most useful if the efficiency of an equal-weighted prior is investment relevant. In many practical cases, a capitalization-weighted prior may be more relevant. In addition, the algorithm is not very stable computationally and is useful primarily for relatively small numbers of assets: Optimizations of 50 or more assets may be infeasible. Frost-Savarino Stein estimation is also very computationally intensive when used in conjunction with Monte Carlo simulation procedures and resampled frontier estimation.

## Covariance Estimation

A simple formula relates the covariance of returns of two securities to their variances or standard deviations and correlation.[14] The covariance matrix is a convenient way of summarizing all the risk estimates

---

[14] The covariance of the return of two assets is the product of their return standard deviations times their correlation.

associated with assets in an MV optimization.[15] The standard deviations in Table 2.3 and the correlations in Table 2.4 provide the information necessary for computing the historic sample covariance matrix for the eight assets.

Asset allocation studies often estimate the sample covariance matrix from historic data, as in Tables 2.3 and 2.4. In contrast, commercial services often use factor models and many advanced statistical techniques to estimate stock and stock portfolio risk. The analysis of equity risk estimation is beyond the scope of this text and is a significant digression from the study of MV optimization.[16] Multivariate equity risk estimation addresses the particular needs of optimizing large institutional portfolios. Although conventional covariance estimation enhancements may be directly useful for asset allocation, they are also applicable to equity risk estimation, factor models, and return forecasting.[17]

Asset managers often express relatively minimal interest in covariance estimation enhancements. The conventional wisdom among asset managers is that risk estimation is a lower-order consideration, particularly with respect to forecasting return. Unfortunately, in the context of MV optimization, conventional wisdom may be in serious error. There are two issues to consider: (1) Is there enough data to estimate the covariance matrix? (2) Are covariance estimation errors dominating the optimization procedure?

Conventional covariance estimation may require a lot of historic data. Unless there are at least as many periods as assets, two problems may arise: The estimates of the sample covariances may be unreliable, and the covariance matrix may be singular or ill conditioned. An ill-conditioned covariance matrix can be a serious cause of MV optimization instability (Michaud 1989a).

Another, subtler source of MV optimization instability results from covariance estimation. As the number of assets increases, the mean estimates increase linearly while the covariance estimates increase quadratically. For a sufficiently large number of assets, the accumulation of covariance estimation error may dominate the optimization pro-

---

[15] The covariance matrix is square with $n$ rows and columns equal to the number of assets. The $i,j$ element is the covariance of the $i$th and $j$th assets. It follows that the $i$th diagonal element is equal to the variance of the $i$th asset.

[16] Early examples include Rosenberg and McKibben (1973), Rosenberg and Guy (1973), and Rosenberg (1974).

[17] The covariance matrix is often part of advanced generalized least squares methods used in risk estimation, factor models, and return forecasting.

cess.[18] Such effects may have an impact on equity portfolio optimizations that use factor models for covariance estimation as well as asset allocation studies that use more conventional methods.

If monthly returns are used, even relatively small optimizations may require more data than is historically available to avoid singularity or ill conditioning. In too many cases, the problems of too little data and the accumulation of estimation errors are unrecognized, leading to unstable optimizations and irrelevant portfolios. Only very recently have Stein covariance estimation methods become available that address some of these important issues.

## Stein Covariance Estimation

Ledoit (1994, 1997) developed Stein estimation methods for the sample covariance matrix. The Ledoit estimator is a general procedure for optimally shrinking the covariance matrix toward a prior.[19]

The Ledoit estimator has many attractive properties. As simulation experiments demonstrate, the estimator significantly improves sample covariance estimation and the stability of MV optimization. Another important benefit is that it is the first procedure to allow estimation of the covariance matrix even if the number of assets is greater than the number of observations. In addition, the procedure is very flexible: Ledoit estimation may be useful with many alternative priors.

Another important Stein estimator of the covariance comes from Stein (1982) and Dey and Srinivasan (1985). Their procedure is a minimax estimator similar in important ways to Ledoit.[20] Using Monte Carlo simulation, Ledoit (1994) finds that both Stein estimators significantly improve sample covariance estimation and the stability of MV optimization.

If the number of assets is small, the benefits of the Ledoit and minimax estimators may be relatively minimal. For the historic data of Tables 2.3 and 2.4, neither estimator significantly alters the sample covariance matrix or the optimization results.[21] Ledoit estimates that the

---

[18] Personal communication from Philippe Jorion, May 1996, based on some preliminary results.

[19] See the appendix in this chapter for further, more technical discussion.

[20] In both cases, the sample covariance shrinks toward a prior. In the Stein-Dey-Srinivasan case, the estimator is minimax; that is, no other estimator has lower worst-case error. This is in contrast to the Ledoit estimator, which uses square error loss (Hilbert-Schmidt or Frobenius norm).

[21] Priors used included the identity, single-index, and capitalization weighting.

benefits of his covariance estimator kick in when the number of assets and periods is on the order of 30.[22] One area of significant application may be to global equity portfolio optimization, where the number of assets can be very large and the number of historic periods of useful data is often small. Because the Ledoit estimator may be useful in situations with minimal historic data, applications to short-term asset allocation may evolve over time.

## Forecasting Stock Risk and Return

Stein covariance estimation may also be useful for asset management by improving regression estimates of equity risk and return forecasts. Generalized least squares (GLS) regression is more powerful and robust in many applications relevant to investment management (Kandel and Stambaugh 1995). In particular, Ledoit shows that his covariance estimator used in the context of GLS regression may significantly change the factor-return relationships observed in some well-known empirical studies.[23]

Other Stein estimators designed for improving the forecast power of linear regression estimation are also available. In particular, the James-Stein linear regression estimator is widely used by many working econometricians.[24]

## Utility Functions and Input Estimation

The reader may have noted that the discussion on optimization input estimation is free of Bayesian priors applied to utility function–based optimization. This may seem surprising because many of the early studies in estimation error and its impact on MV optimization applied Bayesian priors to utility functions.[25] One reason is the problem of utility function specificity discussed in chapter 3. In addition, as Barry (1974) notes, although the optimal portfolio chosen by Bayesian estimation methods applied to utility functions may vary, the efficient frontier composition may be unchanged. Procedures that leave the efficient frontier portfolios unaltered are likely to have limited practical investment value.

---

[22] The benefits depend on the ratio of the assets to periods as well as to the prior.

[23] Ledoit (1994) repeats Fama-French (1992).

[24] Judge et al. (1988, 836–38) discusses Stein rules for multivariate linear regression.

[25] For example Bawa, Brown, and Klein (1979).

### Ad Hoc Estimators

There are a number of ad hoc estimators of the covariance matrix. Perhaps the best known is Sharpe's (1963) single-index model. There are also multi-index and equal-correlation models. Such methods provide simple approaches to estimating risk and the covariance matrix. They may have practical value when the number of observations is small relative to the number of assets and the alternative is a singular covariance matrix. Historically, ad hoc procedures have often been the only ones available for dealing with many limitations of investment data. However, as Ledoit (1994) notes, such procedures may impose arbitrary structure and ignore information available in historic data. The Stein covariance estimation methods are theoretically and intuitively superior. Properly formulated Stein methods ignore neither reasonable structure nor information in historic data. Such estimators weight the prior and data optimally to produce superior risk estimation. Although ad hoc methods have the virtue of simplicity and familiarity, they may be inferior to well-defined Stein estimators, when available.

### Conclusions

Stein estimators represent an important set of procedures for improving the practical value of MV optimization. It is hard to rationalize the continued use of inadmissible estimators for the mean or covariance in practice. It is also increasingly hard to rationalize ad hoc estimators used by many investment practitioners. Stein estimators are available for all optimization parameters. On the other hand, the development of Stein estimators for portfolio optimization is at a relatively early stage. In particular, the identification of the optimal Stein estimator in many practical contexts is generally open. The investment community has a strong interest in the importance of this area of statistical analysis and in encouraging further research.

*Appendix*

# Ledoit Covariance Estimation

*I*f the sample covariance matrix has rank *n*, where *n* equals the number of assets, then the matrix has *n* positive eigenvalues. For the historic data in Tables 2.3 and 2.4, the eight eigenvalues corresponding to the eight asset classes range from 0.23 to 121.6. The eigenvalues of a matrix are often useful in understanding its statistical characteristics.[26]

Ledoit (1994) shows that the conditioning or invertability of the covariance matrix and the resulting stability of the optimization depend on the statistical properties of the eigenvalues of the covariance matrix. The biases of the sample eigenvalues, as in the sample means, are toward too large and too small values. In particular, the ill conditioning of the covariance matrix is attributable to the bias of the small eigenvalues toward zero. The bias increases as the number of assets increases relative to the number of periods. As in the case of the sample means, improved covariance estimation requires shrinking the eigenvalues toward an appropriate prior.

The Ledoit procedure is not a specific estimator. The procedure allows many alternative covariance priors. These include identity matrix, equal correlations, Sharpe's single-index model, K index models, and capitalization weights.

---

[26] For a useful brief introduction to properties of matrices, including eigenvalues and eigenvectors, see Johnson and Wichern (1992, chapter 2).

*Chapter* **9**

# Benchmark Active Asset Allocation

*B*enchmark optimization is a mean-variance (MV) optimization that includes a benchmark return for each asset. A typical benchmark return is the return of an index portfolio. As illustrated in Exhibit 2.2, a benchmark optimization may be based on residual return or the return of an asset minus the return of the benchmark.

Benchmark optimization may dramatically redefine the notion of portfolio efficiency. The value of the procedure depends on the investment relevance of the benchmark prior. In practice, the choice of the benchmark prior is often unambiguous. In many applications, benchmark optimization is the procedure of choice, and classic MV efficiency is inappropriate.

Benchmark optimizations are among the most powerful tools for reducing the instability of classic MV asset allocations and enhancing investment value (Michaud 1989c). The method works by anchoring the optimization to the benchmark. The increase in optimization stability and reliability is often analogous to that which occurs in modern Bayesian statistical methods with a reliable prior.

At least three benchmark optimization frameworks are commonly used by investment practitioners for asset allocation:

1. benchmark- or index-relative

2. implied return

3. economic liability–relative

The first two are active asset allocation frameworks, and they are the focus of this chapter. The third, discussed in chapter 10, is appropriate for defining long-term investment policy.

## Benchmark-Relative Active Asset Allocation

As discussed in chapter 2, benchmark MV optimization (see Exhibit 2.2) is generally the optimization framework of choice for active equity management. Although less used for active asset allocation, benchmark optimization is often no less appropriate.

Assume a benchmark return, such as the return of an index or a manager's performance benchmark. The benchmark return defines a baseline return for each asset in each period. Compute MV optimization inputs based on the difference between asset and benchmark (residual) return. By definition, the benchmark portfolio is MV residual return efficient.[1] Note that benchmark-relative optimization redefines both return and risk.[2] Optimization inputs may include both historic and exogenous forecasts of return.[3]

The data of Tables 2.3 and 2.4 are useful for illustrating the impact of introducing a benchmark prior portfolio into an asset allocation. Assume the index portfolio defined in Table 2.2 as the benchmark portfolio. Table 9.1 provides the monthly means and standard deviations of index-relative return for the eight asset classes and historic data of Tables 2.3 and 2.4. In Table 9.1, France has the highest index-relative average return for the period; Japan and France average return differ only in the fourth significant figure. Note that index-relative risk for Japan is significantly less than for France, a change from the relationships in Tables 2.1 and 2.3.

Exhibit 9.1 provides the index-relative MV efficient frontier, index-relative average returns, and risk for assets and reference portfolios as well as the statistical equivalence region based on 500 simulations. Visually comparing Exhibit 9.1 to Exhibit 4.1 shows significant differences in the implications for efficiency between the two frameworks. In particular, Exhibit 9.1 indicates that many assets and reference portfolios are relatively less active return than return premium efficient. Except

---

[1] The issue of whether the benchmark is or is not MV efficient on an absolute return basis and its implications is discussed further in the section on Roll's (1992) analysis at the end of this chapter.

[2] In the case where benchmark return is index return, there are three equivalent ways of defining index-relative MV optimization. For index-relative returns, either active portfolio weights (sum to zero) or portfolio weights (sum to 1) reach equivalent results because the index has no risk and no return. Alternatively, a traditional portfolio MV optimization based on active weights is also equivalent. This is the approach taken in Roll (1992). Although mathematically elegant, the Roll framework is not convenient for highlighting the Bayesian interpretation of the procedure.

[3] Chapter 11 discusses how to include exogenous expected returns in a benchmark-relative optimization framework.

**Table 9.1:** Monthly Dollar (Net) Index-Relative Returns (Percentages), January 1978–December 1995

|  | Mean | Standard Deviation |
|---|---|---|
| Canada | −0.36 | 4.31 |
| France | 0.13 | 4.90 |
| Germany | −0.22 | 4.81 |
| Japan | 0.13 | 4.63 |
| U.K. | 0.04 | 4.06 |
| U.S. | −0.04 | 3.21 |
| U.S. Bonds | −0.51 | 4.05 |
| Euros | −0.48 | 3.92 |

for the obvious cases—the index, France, and Japan—no other assets or reference portfolios are very close to the active return efficient frontier.

Exhibit 9.2 extends the analysis in Exhibit 9.1 by computing the resampled efficient frontier and 90% sample acceptance region comparable to Exhibit 6.1. The acceptance region shows that neither the current or equal-weighted portfolios, nor the bond assets, are consistent with index-relative efficiency at the 90% confidence level. These results are not surprising; the bond assets are not in the index and the reference portfolios are not designed as active portfolios relative to a global equity market index. As the resampled efficient frontier suggests, only a relatively narrow range of risk may be realistically available for efficient active investment based on the historic data. Statistical analysis illuminates some of the significant investment limitations of the data.

The end points of the index-relative resampled and MV efficient frontiers are of interest. The minimum variance portfolio is the index for both the resampled and efficient frontiers. Because the maximum average return portfolios ignore the index, the maximum average return resampled and MV efficient portfolios are the same as in Table 6.3.

The intermediate index-relative efficient portfolios require further analysis. Table 9.2 provides the statistical analysis of the middle MV

**Exhibit 9.1:** Index-Relative and Statistical Equivalence Region Efficient Frontier

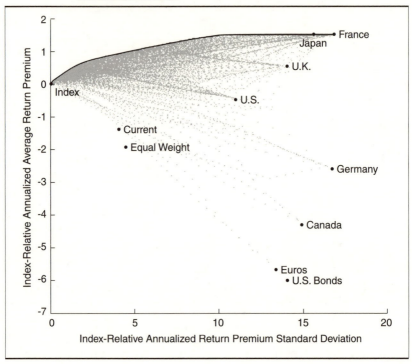

efficient frontier portfolio. The analysis is comparable to that in Table 6.2. The two additional columns in Table 9.2 are the index weights (column 8) and the active weights of the resampled efficient portfolio relative to the index (column 9).

Comparing Table 9.2 to Table 6.2 demonstrates the impact of imposing the efficiency of the index on the optimization. Both the middle index-relative resampled and MV efficient portfolios are near the index. One investment consequence is that the MV and resampled efficient portfolio weights for U.S. and Japanese markets are now statistically significantly different from zero at the 5% significance level. Note also the substantial role change of the bond assets. Because bonds are not part of the index, they are not statistically significantly different from zero at the 5% level and are not a component of the middle portfolio index-relative efficient frontier. The notion of index-relative efficiency is much less ambiguous than in the return premium case. This result is consistent with the increase in statistical power associated with Bayesian priors represented by benchmark optimization methods.

**Exhibit 9.2:** Index-Relative Efficient Frontiers, Resampled Frontier, and 90 Percent Acceptance Region

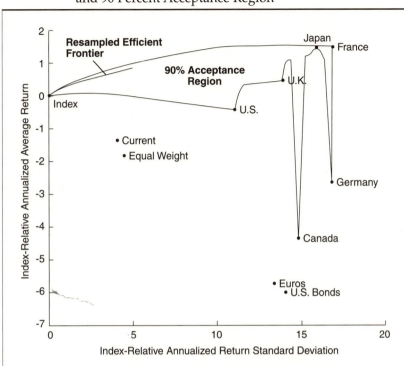

Table 9.3 provides a simultaneous 90% confidence interval analysis of the simulated efficient middle portfolios comparable to Table 7.3. When compared to Table 7.3, the impact of index-relative efficiency can be seen not only in the significantly lower upper bounds for the bond assets but also the narrower upper range of allocations for other assets, such as U.S. equities.

The results confirm that benchmark-relative optimization may impose investment-relevant structure on the optimization process. To the extent that the prior is a valid reflection of investment objectives, benchmark optimization reduces the likelihood of investment-irrelevant portfolios.

## Implied-Return Asset Allocation

Implied returns are an alternative approach to defining a benchmark asset allocation framework for active management. The implied-return procedure is due to Fisher (1975) and Sharpe (1974). Given an

**Table 9.2:** Statistical Analysis: Index-Relative Middle Efficient Portfolio

| Asset | Resampled Efficient Portfolio | 5th Percentile | 95th Percentile | Standard Error | T-statistic | MV Efficient Portfolio | Index Portfolio | Active Resampled Portfolio |
|-------|------|------|------|------|------|------|------|------|
| Canada | 0.01 | 0 | 0.07 | 0.04 | 0.27 | 0 | 0.05 | -0.04 |
| France | 0.16 | 0 | 0.39 | 0.13 | 1.28 | 0.18 | 0.10 | 0.06 |
| Germany | 0.04 | 0 | 0.19 | 0.07 | 0.57 | 0 | 0.10 | -0.06 |
| Japan | 0.33 | 0.14 | 0.55 | 0.12 | 2.78 | 0.34 | 0.30 | 0.03 |
| U.K. | 0.15 | 0 | 0.37 | 0.13 | 1.18 | 0.14 | 0.10 | 0.03 |
| U.S. | 0.31 | 0.1 | 0.53 | 0.13 | 2.3 | 0.34 | 0.35 | -0.04 |
| U.S. Bonds | 0 | 0 | 0 | 0.01 | 0.13 | 0 | 0 | 0 |
| Euros | 0 | 0 | 0 | 0.02 | 0.07 | 0 | 0 | 0 |

*Note*: MV efficient portfolio mean = 0.69%; standard deviation = 2.19%. Resampled efficient portfolio mean = 0.47%; standard deviation = 1.75%.

**Table 9.3:** 90 Percent Simultaneous Confidence Intervals:
Index-Relative Middle Efficient Portfolio

|  | Lower Bound | Resampled Efficient Portfolio | Upper Bound |
|---|---|---|---|
| Canada | 0 | 0.01 | 0.40 |
| France | 0 | 0.17 | 0.40 |
| Germany | 0 | 0.04 | 0.32 |
| Japan | 0.08 | 0.32 | 0.56 |
| U.K. | 0 | 0.13 | 0.48 |
| U.S. | 0 | 0.31 | 0.64 |
| U.S. Bonds | 0 | 0 | 0.40 |
| Euros | 0.04 | 0 | 0.44 |

*Note:* Accurate to within +/− 0.08 range.

MV efficient portfolio prior and the sample covariance matrix, a reverse optimization finds the implied or benchmark returns for each asset.[4] By definition, the implied returns and the covariance matrix lead to an efficient frontier that includes the portfolio prior. The implied returns are a baseline return for each asset. In applications, the efficient portfolio prior is generally a representative market portfolio.

Black and Litterman (1992) advocate the implied-return framework for active asset allocation. One rationale is that return estimates are typically less reliable than risk estimates. This reliability mismatch may be a significant source of the instability of an optimization (Michaud 1989a). In addition, an asset allocation framework that implies an inefficient market or benchmark in the absence of active return forecasts may be unsuitable. The implied-return procedure solves these problems by finding passive or neutral expected returns that are consistent with the sample covariance matrix and the assumed MV efficiency of the portfolio prior. In contrast to the benchmark-relative optimization framework, the benchmark return in the implied-return

---

[4] The backward optimization formula for computing implied returns is simply the covariance matrix times the MV efficient portfolio weight vector.

**Exhibit 9.3:** Implied Return Premium Efficient Frontier

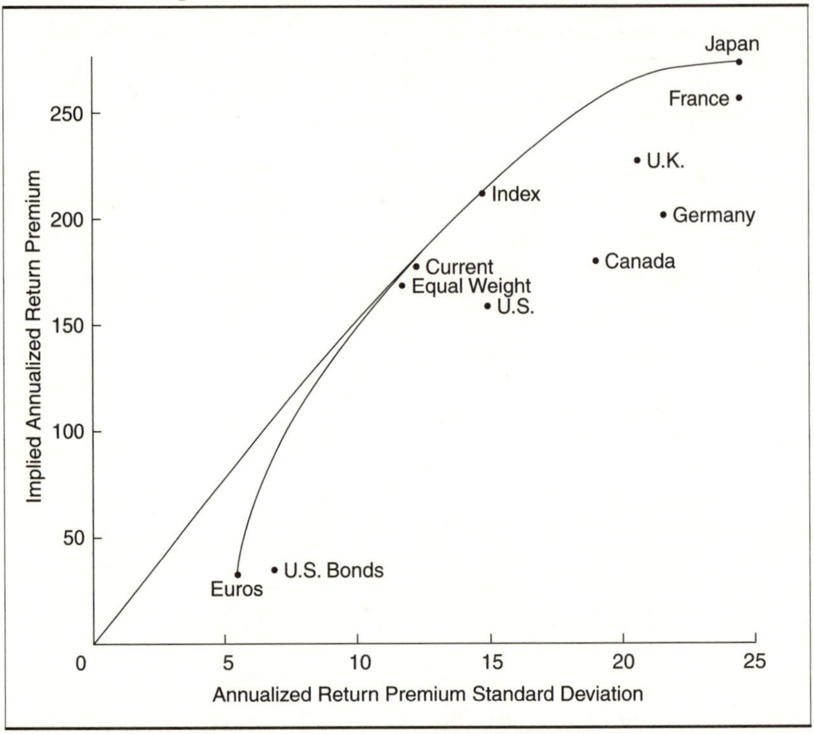

framework is additive and affects only the estimation of return. The new expected return for each asset is expected residual or active return *plus* the implied return.[5]

The implied-return procedure imposes interesting structure on the optimization. The implied returns are interpretable as average return premiums (see Table 2.3). The efficient portfolio prior is the maximum Sharpe ratio portfolio in the absence of active expected returns. In the implied return procedure, risk is unchanged.

Exhibit 9.3 shows the implied return efficient frontier using the co-variance data in Tables 2.3 and 2.4 and the MV efficiency prior of the index portfolio in Table 2.2. The tangent line drawn from the origin shows that the index is on the efficient frontier and is the maximum Sharpe ratio portfolio. Comparing the results with Exhibit 2.5 shows that the implied return procedure fundamentally alters the relative relationship of

---

[5] Chapter 11 discusses further how to mix active returns with historic estimated data.

many assets and portfolios with respect to each other and to the efficient portfolio set. Exhibit 9.3, however, has significant unintuitive investment characteristics. The estimated implied return premiums, which range from 0% to 300% annualized, are inconsistent with the scale of the standard deviation of annualized monthly returns or investment intuition.

As Fisher (1975) and Sharpe (1974) show, the implied return premiums are unique up to a linear transformation.[6] Consequently, linearly rescaling the implied returns so that they are consistent with the scale of monthly data does not change the composition of the implied return efficient frontier. Exhibit 9.4 displays the implied returns linearly scaled so that the spread of the maximum and minimum values are equal to that of the historic monthly return premiums and consistent with a zero riskless rate. Rescaling allows a more direct comparison with previous results.

## Comparing Implied-Return and Benchmark-Relative Frontiers

It is interesting to compare the benchmark-relative efficient frontiers in Exhibits 9.2 and 9.4. Both use the same historic data and efficient portfolio prior. In both cases the index is MV efficient. However, the efficient frontiers and many asset-relative valuations are not the same. To further understanding, it is useful to examine the differences with respect to French and Japanese equities. In the classic sense Japan and France are nearly MV identical. In the index-relative Exhibit 9.2, Japan has less risk than France, whereas in Exhibit 9.4, Japan has more expected return. Because Japan is more correlated to the index, it has more expected return in an implied-return framework and less risk in an index-relative return framework. In both benchmark optimizations, Japan has increased in attractiveness relative to France but in different ways. Changes in other assets have somewhat similar explanations.

## Scaling and Implied Returns

The investment value of the implied return procedure should be of some concern. The return premium covariance matrix is the sole source of historic information. As noted in chapter 8, the sample covariance matrix is also prone to estimation error and biased toward ill conditioning. It is not necessarily a better source of information on which to base the optimization.

---

[6] More accurately, a positive multiplicative linear transformation.

**Exhibit 9.4:** Scaled Implied Return Premium Efficient Frontier

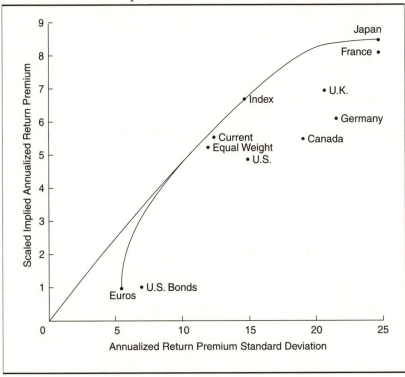

The nonuniqueness of the implied returns leads to further issues. Efficient asset allocations based on active and implied returns may change dramatically simply by changing the scale of the implied returns. Suppose two assets with active expected returns of 0.5% and –1.0% and implied returns of 1.5% and 2%. The active expected returns do not have an arbitrary scale. They presumably reflect the return on average associated with the forecast. However, the implied returns may not have a unique scale. Multiplying the implied returns by 4 inverts the rank of the expected returns (implied plus active) of the two assets and changes the optimal asset allocation significantly. The example shows that the implied-return optimization framework is highly scale dependent and may not be unique.

The question of interest is whether the scale-dependent character of the implied-return procedure limits or invalidates its investment usefulness. In addition, do implied returns have any inherent investment content? Is the currently fashionable procedure of comparing implied returns with average historic returns justifiable? What assumptions, if any, are necessary for implied returns to have useful investment information?

The investment value of the procedure rests on whether there exists a natural or unique scale for implied returns. If there is no unique scale, the asset allocations and implied returns are nonunique and arbitrary, and the procedure may have little investment content.

Black and Litterman (1992) have proposed to equate the return of the efficient portfolio prior with the equilibrium return of a "market" portfolio.[7] In this view, if the portfolio prior represents the "market," if the market is in equilibrium, and if market return has a stationary distribution, then long-term return premium data may be useful for estimating equilibrium market returns. Under these conditions, the long-term return data may define a natural scale for the implied return of the market portfolio and therefore for the assets and asset allocation. In this case, the MV asset allocation may be unique and well defined, and the implied asset returns may be comparable to actual returns.

The natural scale issue for the implied-return framework presents some significant practical considerations, including

1. how to define the "market" portfolio,

2. the reasonableness of the market equilibrium assumption,

3. the validity of the stationary return distribution assumption,

4. the availability of appropriate long-term data for estimation, and

5. the unambiguity of the return premium estimate.

Note that an efficient global market portfolio may include a number of asset classes, such as real estate, fixed income, and venture capital in foreign markets, for which there is very limited reliable empirical data. The ambiguity of the return premium estimate is also a significant consideration. Suppose a long-term return premium estimate from 2% to 10% annualized. The ambiguity of the resulting MV optimized asset allocations based on this range of implied returns may not be that much different from the ambiguity resulting from traditional MV optimization.

---

[7] The specific proposal in Black and Litterman (1992) for defining a natural scale for the implied returns, the "universal hedging" equilibrium, includes the universal currency hedging formula that all investors may want to use in equilibrium (Black 1989). Their argument involves similar but more restrictive additional empirical issues and assumptions (see Black and Litterman 1992, fn. 9).

There are other issues. Historic risk estimates may not always be an accurate reflection of return expectations. In addition, the implied-return framework may pose some special limitations for forecasting return. Because return in the implied-return framework is a function of risk, a forecast $\alpha$ based on the risk, rather than the return, history of a security may require nonstandard econometric estimation techniques.[8]

Alternatively, index-relative asset allocation is not scale dependent. The procedure may be superior if the benchmark is not a market portfolio, if the market is not in equilibrium or if the long-term return premium estimate for the market is ambiguous. In addition, active return forecasting may be more reliable.

Benchmark-relative efficiency may be a less error prone and more widely applicable framework for active asset allocation. Roll (1992) presents a critique of the index-relative framework and discusses a number of caveats. Holding Roll's caveats in mind, on balance, benchmark-relative efficiency may be the active asset allocation framework of choice in many applications.

## Roll's Analysis

Roll (1992) provides a theoretical analysis of the index-relative efficient frontier framework. In particular, he shows that many portfolios may dominate index-relative efficient portfolios. His result is not surprising because index-relative efficiency generally leads to different solutions from classic MV efficiency. Roll's concern is that the convenience of an index-relative efficient frontier framework for institutional asset management may come at too high a price in terms of suboptimal investment.

Roll raises important issues on the relationship of index and index-relative efficiency. If the index is not MV efficient in the conventional sense, then positive index-relative performance may be an artifact of an insufficiently MV efficient index. Consequently, the MV efficiency of the index is important.

At a minimum, Roll's analysis indicates the importance of attending to the investment integrity of benchmarks.[9] The theoretical limitations of the index-relative framework diminish as the MV efficiency and representativeness of the benchmark increases. As Roll also notes in his conclusion (1992, 19–20), the problem with concern of the suboptimality of the index-relative MV efficiency framework may need

---

[8] I am indebted to Robert Michaud for this observation.

[9] See also Kandel and Stambaugh (1995) and Roll and Ross (1994).

to be balanced against the impact of estimation error on MV optimization in the classic framework. As previous analyses have shown, the ambiguity of traditional MV efficiency is very severe in many cases of practical application and the likelihood of investment-irrelevant efficient portfolios is very real. The benefit of the benchmark-relative framework is the imposition of a prior on optimized portfolio structure that is consistent with investment objectives and enhances the likelihood of practical and relevant optimized portfolios. Although Roll's cautionary analysis is interesting and useful, the problems of MV optimization error maximization appear to dominate the potential limitations of index-relative efficiency in many cases of practical interest.

## Additional Procedures

Many other procedures may significantly enhance the practical value of the benchmark-relative framework. In particular, chapter 11 addresses the important topic of rigorously mixing active return forecasts with historic return data.

# Chapter 10

# Investment Policy and Economic Liabilities

*I*nvestment policy defines a fund's expected long-term average asset allocation. For many fund trustees, appropriately defining investment policy is a major investment priority and a significant fiduciary responsibility. An investment policy study may often consist of substantial expenditures of time and capital. Although the degree of importance may be controversial, a broad consensus in the investment community holds that investment policy is at least as important as any other investment decision.[1]

Conceptually, mean-variance (MV) optimization is a natural framework for defining investment policy. Intuitively, MV optimizations based on long-term historic return data appear to be the most obvious way to define an optimal long-term asset allocation. Beyond the problems imposed by MV optimization, investment policy studies have additional practical limitations.

## Misusing Mean-Variance Efficiency

An MV optimization framework for defining investment policy is very vulnerable to overmanagement and misuse. Because of instability, MV optimizations are often inconsistent with investment intuition and institutional perceptions. There is often a great deal of pressure to find acceptable optimized investment policy allocations. Many constraints and assumptions, rationalized as reflecting institutional objectives and constraints, may become part of the optimization process. All too often, the investment policy MV optimization reflects little more

---

[1] In the controversy concerning Brinson et al. (1986) and the follow-on investigation of Hensel et al. (1991), there is nevertheless agreement that investment policy is a key investment decision.

than a priori constraints and prejudices. Consequently, MV efficiency may provide a veneer of scientific respectability for rationalizing an essentially ad hoc process.

Because of the importance of the problem, and the limitations of the traditional MV efficiency framework, several alternative approaches for defining investment policy have been proposed. Some of the most popular use Monte Carlo asset-liability financial planning methods with liability modeling. As discussed in chapter 3, however, asset-liability financial planning methods also have limitations that are no less serious than those of MV optimization. Is it possible to enhance the MV efficiency framework so that it is useful for defining investment policy?

## Economic Liability Models

The author has found an MV efficiency framework enhanced with benchmark optimization techniques useful for defining investment policy in many cases (Michaud 1989c). The procedure requires an investment policy relevant prior in the form of an economic model of fund liabilities or obligations (Michaud 1989b).

The notion of an "economic" liability is a relatively novel one. The term *economic* highlights the substantive differences that may exist between such models and actuarial approaches for defining liabilities, particularly with respect to defined benefit pension plans.

The objective of economic liability modeling is to describe how fund values and obligations interact and change dynamically in time. The economic liability model reflects changes in the fund's obligations as a function of changes in economic factors and asset returns. The economic model may also be a function of the level of assets and liabilities, when they are not equal. The success of the procedure depends critically on a valid model of liability risk. Similar to the impact of introducing a benchmark-relative return prior, an economic liability benchmark-relative optimization may radically alter the investment character and improve the investment value of MV investment policy optimizations.

The critical step is to define an appropriate model of period-by-period changes in the capital value of fund obligations as a baseline return for each asset. After that, investment policy benchmark optimization is straightforward. The economic liability returns form the basis of the benchmark-relative optimization parameter inputs and computation of the MV efficient frontier.

## An Example: Endowment Fund Investment Policy

Endowment fund investment policy studies often provide convenient examples of benchmark-relative economic liability optimization. In many cases, simple economic liability models reflect changes in fund obligations and baseline returns for the fund. For example, an endowment fund's investment objective may require maintaining purchasing power over time. Meeting the inflation rate is a convenient interpretation of the fund's obligations. In this case, the historic inflation rate is the benchmark-relative liability return in each period.

A college endowment fund's investment objectives may not be as simple as meeting the inflation rate, however. One alternative is to define the fund's obligations in terms of maintaining a college's competitiveness among similar schools in attracting students. For example, the fund may serve as a vehicle for financing student aid. Then an appropriate economic liability model of benchmark return may include historic changes in student costs, including tuition, fees, and room and board.[2]

## Pension Liabilities and Benchmark Optimization

Investment policy studies for corporate final average pay defined benefit pension plans are probably the case of most institutional interest. Although it may seem reasonably straightforward to define economic liability models for endowment funds, foundations, or even individuals, it may seem much less so for defined benefit pension plans. For many fund trustees and consultants, pension plan liabilities are inextricably associated with actuarial estimation methods. To the extent that economic liability benchmark optimization is a universal framework for defining investment policy, it must be applicable to defined benefit pension plans.

The rest of this chapter explains how benchmark-relative optimization with economic liability modeling can be applied to defining investment policy for defined benefit pension plans. In the process, I address the economic nature of pension plan liabilities, a topic of substantial interest to many institutional investors. Some limitations of actuarial methods for defining investment policy are also covered.

---

[2] An investment policy study conducted by the author in summer 1996 for the Massachusetts College of Art Foundation in Boston included similar objectives.

## Limitations of Actuarial Liability Estimation

Are actuarially estimated pension liabilities useful in defining investment policy? It may surprise many outside the actuarial profession to know that pension liability estimation is not the primary focus of the defined benefit actuarial estimation process.

The actuarial estimation process of pension plan obligations is a tool of corporate financial management. The design objective of an actuarial valuation is to estimate required plan contributions for the orderly funding of current and emerging plan obligations. In many cases, the corporate funding objective is to maintain pension costs as a fixed percent of payroll. Actuarial pension liabilities are constructs for estimating plan contributions. Many actuarial assumptions are not economically realistic. Actuarial pension liabilities can be made larger or smaller depending on corporate funding needs and objectives, including whether the corporation prefers to pay benefits now or later. Misperceptions of liability risk, including the illusion of minimal period-by-period variability, are associated with the smoothing of variability endemic to the actuarial estimation process and the tradition of occasional in-depth actuarial valuations.

For investment policy planning, actuarial methods may be useful primarily for approximating the current capital value of plan benefits and funding status. Current funding status may be important for defining investment policy, particularly when plan underfunding is significant and plan termination is a serious consideration. Actuarial methods have severe limitations for reflecting pension liability risk.

### Economic Pension Liabilities

Economic pension liability models depend on an understanding of the economic nature of pension plan obligations. The variability of pension liabilities depends primarily on economic factors that are generally outside the scope of actuarial methods. A key to understanding the risks of pension liabilities is to recognize that there are two types of pension liabilities: current, or accrued, and future, or expected. For defining investment policy, pension liability risk dominates the investment policy decision.

### Current Pension Liabilities

Plan termination obligations are a first-order consideration for many plan sponsors. This is because plan termination is often a significant corporate consideration, particularly if the firm is in financial distress. Under U.S. law, vested pension benefits are financial obligations of the plan and of the firm, whether or not the plan terminates. The accrued benefit obligation (ABO) defines the capital value at market interest rates associated with plan termination benefits.

Plan termination liabilities are associated with retirees and the vested benefits of current employees. Assume a current employee with 10 years of vested service and 10 years to retirement. If plan termination occurs, the plan has the financial obligation to pay the accumulated plan benefits associated with 10 years of service and current final average salary 10 years from now. The promised benefit in this case is similar to a long-term bond with a delayed first payment period. The plan benefits for retirees have no delay in payment period. The benefit payments of accrued or current plan obligations under plan termination are highly predictable cash flows derivable from mortality tables. Such liabilities are primarily interest rate sensitive and financially similar to a portfolio of short- and long-term bonds.

### Total and Variable Pension Liabilities

Suppose that the firm is ongoing and plan termination is not a significant consideration. In this case, there are additional plan liabilities. Consider the vested employee with 10 years of service and 10 years until retirement. Suppose that the employee remains with the firm until retirement. In this case, the employee's 10 years of current service is associated with a pension benefit that depends on final average pay 10 years from now. The capital value of a benefit that depends on final average pay 10 years from now is likely to be significantly greater than the plan benefit evaluated with current final average pay. Consequently, the value of funds that are required to consider the plan fully funded for all the promised benefits, current and likely, may be much larger than that associated with plan termination. Because the purpose of the pension fund is to assist the firm in providing orderly funding of plan benefits, proper planning includes estimation of expected or emerging benefits associated with the ongoing functioning of the plan. The capital value of the difference between termination and total liabilities may be significant, especially for senior officers of the firm.

Define the estimated capital value at a given point in time of all current and expected plan benefits as the total benefit obligation (TBO) of the pension plan. It is convenient to define the variable benefit obligation (VBO) of the pension plan as the difference between the TBO and ABO:

$$VBO = TBO - ABO$$

The VBO is the expected pension benefit component of total pension liability. Estimates of required funding levels and considerations of the risk characteristics of pension obligations often ignore the VBO.

## Economic Significance of Variable Liabilities

Is the VBO a significant portion of the total pension obligation? For companies in mature industries, the VBO may be a relatively minor portion of total plan obligations. This is because most pension obligations may be associated with employees near or at retirement. On the other hand, for fast-growing companies, the VBO may be the dominant portion of plan liabilities. One estimate is that the VBO is typically 70% of the ABO (Michaud 1989c).

A plan sponsor has the option of terminating the pension plan. Does this make VBO liabilities unimportant? In plan termination, the VBO has zero capital value by definition, and the TBO equals the ABO. Consequently, the view may be that only assets for funding ABO liabilities are required. Such arguments ignore some fundamental economic truths.

By definition, a pension plan is deferred wages. The pension plan is part of the total wage and fringe benefit package associated with employment at the firm. Terminating the pension plan implies a reduction in total compensation paid by the firm to its employees. A firm that terminates the plan and wants to remain in business will have to be competitive for human capital. In general, this means that the firm has to pay the equivalent capital value of the terminated benefits, probably in the form of current wages. Consequently, there may be no economic benefit to the firm purely from plan termination. The firm may also have to deal with poor employee morale if perceptions of diminished total compensation are prevalent.

A significant economic disadvantage attaches to plan termination for the ongoing firm: Contributions to qualified pension plans, up to a specified limit, are tax advantaged by U.S. law. By terminating the plan, the firm may give up a considerable economic benefit that may cost much more than its equivalent capital value in total compensation to employees.

Plan termination makes economic sense primarily in the context of substantial financial distress and significant concern for the firm's viability. In this case, the economic value of terminating the plan may be worth the likely near-term decrease in competitiveness for human capital or longer-term increase in total compensation required. For a competitive ongoing firm, the VBO is very much an economic reality, whether or not the plan terminates. In many cases, proper investment policy planning requires consideration of both components of total plan liabilities. Contrary to popular perceptions, in the light of tax implications, a defined benefit pension plan is not a corporate liability but a U.S. government–sponsored asset for promoting corporate competitiveness.

## Economic Characteristics of Variable Liabilities

The economic risk characteristics of VBO liabilities are generally very different from the ABO. ABO liabilities have fixed-income risk characteristics that are highly sensitive to interest rates. In contrast, VBO liabilities may often have equity risk characteristics and may not be particularly interest rate sensitive (Michaud 1989b). These fundamental differences have important implications for defining an appropriate defined benefit pension plan investment policy.

VBO risk is associated with the business risks of the firm and its ability to grow and compete for markets and human capital over time. Unexpected changes in VBO liabilities and the firm's payroll are closely associated. Unexpected economic factors that positively affect firm growth are likely to lead to a lower withdrawal rate, larger-than-anticipated salary increases, and unanticipated increases in the workforce, leading to an unexpected increase in firm payroll and VBO liability. Conversely, unexpected economic factors that adversely affect firm growth are likely to have the opposite impact on withdrawal rates and salary and workforce growth, leading to an unexpected decrease in payroll and VBO liability. Consequently, VBO risk is closely linked to regional, national, and global economic risk factors. In some cases, VBO risk may be highly correlated with domestic and global equity market returns and largely unrelated to interest rate risk.[3]

The implications of modeling pension liability risk with economic risk factors can have a dramatic impact on defining investment policy. For example, a VBO with equity risk characteristics may imply that a well-diversified equity portfolio is the low-risk asset allocation of choice, a significant inversion of conventional perceptions.[4] Local and

---

[3] Michaud (1989b) provides an example.

[4] Note that this conclusion is impossible with actuarial liability methods, where the rationalization for equities rests on presumed long-term return benefits as opposed to period-by-period risk characteristics. The example provides further illustration of the critical limitations of actuarial methods for defining investment policy.

**Exhibit 10.1:** Liability-Relative and Statistical Equivalence Region Efficient Frontier

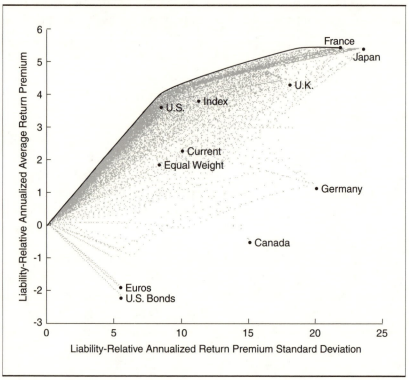

global economic risk factors that affect variable liabilities are often very different from those that affect fixed cash flow securities.

## An Example: Economic Liability Pension Investment Policy

Defining investment policy for a defined benefit pension plan typically involves extensive investigation into the nature of the firm's business risks, the level of current plan liabilities, and the thoughtful use of historic asset returns and economic data. The following discussion provides a very simple example of the benchmark-relative economic liability optimization framework for defining pension plan investment policy.

Suppose that the total pension plan liability consists of 60% ABO and 40% VBO and that the plan is fully funded.[5] Also, assume that U.S. bond

---

[5] Full funding here means that the capital value of the fund equals the TBO. See Michaud (1989c) for benchmark optimization under more general funding assumptions.

**Exhibit 10.2:** Liability-Relative Efficient Frontier, Resampling Efficient Frontier, and 90 Percent Acceptance Region

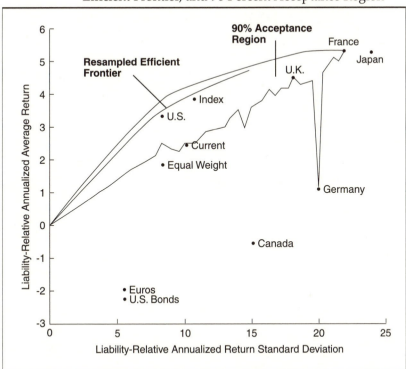

returns model the ABO, and U.S. equity returns model the VBO. Finally, suppose that the historic period and asset return data in Tables 2.3 and 2.4 reflect an appropriate scenario for examining investment policy.

Exhibits 10.1 and 10.2 show the benchmark-relative optimization efficient frontier that results from the simple economic liability model of pension liabilities and historic asset return data.[6] Exhibit 10.1 provides the efficient frontier and statistical equivalence region comparable to Exhibit 4.1. Exhibit 10.2 provides the resampled efficient frontier and 90% sample acceptance region comparable to Exhibit 6.1.

Comparing Exhibits 10.1 and 10.2 to Exhibits 4.1 and 6.1, U.S. stocks are closer to and U.S. bonds are further from the liability-relative efficient frontier. Note that the current portfolio is barely within the liability-relative 90% acceptance region, while the equal-weighted portfolio is not.

---

[6] The pension liability model has primarily illustrative value as a paradigm of the basic modeling process and is unlikely to apply to any real firm.

**Table 10.1:** Statistical Analysis: Middle Liability-Relative Efficient Portfolio

| Asset | Resampled Efficient Portfolio | 5th Percentile | 95th Percentile | Standard Error | T-statistic | MV Efficient Portfolio | Liability Weight | Active Resampled Portfolio |
|---|---|---|---|---|---|---|---|---|
| Canada | 0.01 | 0 | 0.02 | 0.03 | 0.21 | 0 | 0 | 0.01 |
| France | 0.06 | 0 | 0.28 | 0.09 | 0.65 | 0.04 | 0 | 0.07 |
| Germany | 0.02 | 0 | 0.16 | 0.07 | 0.42 | 0 | 0 | 0.03 |
| Japan | 0.10 | 0 | 0.34 | 0.11 | 0.85 | 0.09 | 0 | 0.09 |
| U.K. | 0.07 | 0 | 0.28 | 0.1 | 0.66 | 0.02 | 0 | 0.06 |
| U.S. | 0.52 | 0.12 | 0.68 | 0.17 | 3.0 | 0.63 | 0.4 | 0.12 |
| U.S. Bonds | 0.13 | 0 | 0.33 | 0.13 | 1.01 | 0.21 | 0.6 | −0.52 |
| Euros | 0.09 | 0 | 0.38 | 0.14 | 0.64 | 0 | 0 | 0.09 |

*Note:* Efficient portfolio mean = 2.44%; standard deviation = 5.16%. Resampled efficient portfolio mean = 2.40%; standard deviation = 5.46%.

**Table 10.2:** 90 Percent Simultaneous Confidence Intervals:
Middle Liability-Relative Efficient Portfolio

| | Lower Bound | Resampled Efficient Portfolio | Upper Bound |
|---|---|---|---|
| Canada | 0 | 0.01 | 0.42 |
| France | 0 | 0.07 | 0.36 |
| Germany | 0 | 0.03 | 0.36 |
| Japan | 0 | 0.09 | 0.36 |
| U.K. | 0 | 0.06 | 0.42 |
| U.S. | 0 | 0.52 | 0.96 |
| U.S. Bonds | 0 | 0.13 | 0.60 |
| Euros | 0.04 | 0.09 | 0.70 |

*Note:* Accurate to within +/− 0.06 range.

A comparison of the end points of the resampled versus MV efficient frontier portfolios is similar to that in the index-relative case in chapter 9. The minimum variance point is the benchmark-return or economic liability model in both cases. The maximum average return portfolios ignore the benchmark, and the maximum average return MV and resampled efficient portfolios are the same as in Table 6.3. In general, an economic liability model need not consist solely of asset classes, and an asset allocation with zero liability-relative variance may not exist.

Further study of the intermediate points on the resampled and MV efficient liability-relative frontiers is of interest. Table 10.1 provides a statistical analysis of the middle liability-relative efficient frontier portfolio similar to Table 6.2. Table 10.2 provides the associated simultaneous 90% confidence intervals, similar to Table 7.3. For convenience of analysis, Table 10.1 also provides the liability weights in column 8 and the liability-relative active weights of the resampled efficient frontier portfolio in column 9.

Comparing Table 10.1 to Table 6.2 shows the impact of including the economic liability benchmark in the optimization. Table 10.1 shows that U.S. equities are now a statistically significant asset allocation at the 5% significance level. Note that Euros play a less but still important role in funding the liability. As in previous cases, the resampled efficient portfolio has nearly uniformly less extreme portfolio weights than the MV efficient portfolio in column 5 in Table 10.1. Although the benchmark process reduces ambiguity relative to classic MV efficiency, the simplicity of the liability model leads to less striking results than in the index-relative case in chapter 9.

## Conclusion

Economic liability-relative optimization, performed appropriately, is often a significant tool for enhancing the value of MV investment policy studies. In spite of its simplicity, the example indicates that a benchmark-relative economic liability framework may substantially alter the character of the MV optimization as well as its statistical characteristics.

As a practical matter, economic liability risk modeling may not be a simple process. Most critically, particularly in the case of defined benefit pension plans, it may require abandoning basic misconceptions of funding and plan liability risk. The key to the success of the procedure is to define a relevant and appropriate economic liability model of fund liabilities. On the positive side, unlike actuarial approaches, fund trustees and corporate officers often find an economic liability approach to investment policy planning an attractive, institutionally meaningful process.

Many applications of economic liability modeling remain to be developed. Only a few examples of economic liability studies exist.[7] Many issues are open, and extensive research is required to solve specific applications.

---

[7] An early example is the benchmark-relative economic liability investment policy study conducted by the author for the Ameritech Corporation, summer 1989.

# Chapter 11

# Return Forecasts
# and Mixed Estimation

*R*eturn forecasts are a natural part of most applications of port-folio optimization in asset management. In active equity management, portfolio optimization and risk management services generally assume that the manager has forecasts of expected active returns available as inputs. For active asset allocation, the manager typically has views on asset returns that modify or replace historic return estimates. For investment policy studies, asset return views usually modify or replace long-term return estimates so that optimization inputs are consistent with current expectations of long-term economic trends and changes in markets. Clearly, return forecasts are a central part of mean-variance (MV) optimization in practice.

This chapter addresses the issue of rigorously integrating exogenous forecasts of return with historic data for asset management. Rigorous methods may significantly improve the return forecasts and the investment value of MV portfolio optimization.

## Asset Allocation and Ad Hoc Inputs

In many asset allocation studies, the optimization inputs are a combination of exogenous forecasts of return and the sample covariance matrix of historic returns. For example, return forecasts may replace the sample means in Table 2.3. The new optimization inputs may consist of the revised Table 2.3 data and the original data in Table 2.4.

Unfortunately, the ad hoc procedure of replacing sample means with return forecasts has no theoretical justification. It is also one of the most significant sources of MV optimization instability and asset allocation irrelevance. In many cases, the returns are not consistent with historic asset variability and interrelationships represented by the sample covariance. In addition, the procedure ignores any uncertainty or level of reliability of the forecast. For an optimization to be stable, the inputs have to have internal consistency.

## Mixed Estimation Forecasts

Ad hoc procedures for including forecast returns in an asset allocation are hard to justify. Rigorous statistical methods for using exogenous forecasts of return with historic data have been available for a number of years. Theil and Goldberger (1961) worked out a linear regression procedure for rigorously mixing forecast returns and uncertainty with historic data.[1] Black and Litterman (1992) provide a similar formula for MV asset allocation.

Theil-Goldberger mixed estimation assumes that the return forecasts and historic return estimates are independent. The independence requirement in mixed estimation puts into focus the necessary exogenous character of return forecasts. In many practical cases, managers may find it difficult to develop return forecasts that are completely independent of the historic return optimization inputs. However, the benefits of the procedure increase to the extent that the return forecasts satisfy the independence assumption. An organization's ability to produce return forecasts that satisfy mixed estimation assumptions are likely to improve with experience.

## Mixed Estimation Asset Allocation Inputs

In a mixed estimation asset allocation, historic return inputs (sample means and covariances) are mixed with the return forecasts, assumed standard errors of the return forecasts, and relative reliability estimates to produce the mixed estimate returns. The mixed estimate returns and sample covariance are the new inputs into the MV asset allocation. The procedure is very general and is applicable, with some modifications, to most asset allocation frameworks of practical interest.

## Index-Relative Active Asset Allocation

As an illustration of mixed estimation MV asset allocation, consider the index-relative framework described in chapter 9. The data in Table 11.1 illustrate the key inputs and results of the mixed estimation procedure. The first line presents the analysts' exogenous forecasts of

---

[1] See Theil (1971) for an authoritative and comprehensive discussion.

**Table 11.1:** Mixed Estimation with Index-Relative Returns: Alphas and Historic Monthly Means (Percentages)

|            | Alpha | Index-Relative Means | Mixed Estimate |
|------------|-------|----------------------|----------------|
| Canada     | 0.00  | −0.36                | −0.32          |
| France     | 0.10  | 0.13                 | 0.16           |
| Germany    | −0.20 | −0.22                | −0.32          |
| Japan      | −0.20 | 0.13                 | −0.01          |
| U.K.       | 0.00  | 0.04                 | 0.05           |
| U.S.       | 0.20  | −0.04                | 0.06           |
| U.S. Bonds | 0.00  | −0.51                | −0.50          |
| Euros      | 0.00  | −0.48                | −0.48          |

monthly index-relative active return (alpha): 0.2% for U.S. equities, 0.1% for France, and −0.2% for Japan and Germany, no information for other markets. The second line presents the historic index-relative average returns from Table 9.1. The third line in Table 11.1 displays the Theil-Goldberger-Black-Litterman mixed estimate returns. The analysis assumes that the alphas and historic return estimates are equally reliable and that the standard errors of the forecasts are the same as the historic estimates. The mixed return estimates show how the forecasts and historic data mix optimally under the assumptions.[2]

Exhibit 11.1 shows the impact of the mixed estimates on the original asset returns and efficient frontier. The top curve from the right is the mixed estimate efficient frontier. The results show that the right arm of the mixed estimate frontier has rotated upward to reflect a higher return forecast in France, while the lower segment has less return.

The results in Table 11.1 are a simple illustration of the mixed estimation technique. The hallmark of the procedure is its flexibility.[3] In

---

[2] To avoid singularity, one simple approach is to use the return premium covariance matrix from Tables 2.3 and 2.4 for the matrix $\Sigma$ in (8) in the appendix of Black and Litterman (1992). The historic average returns and diagonal variances for $\pi$ and $\Omega$ are from Table 9.1.

[3] The level of certainty may also be set to more than a single period of historic data. See the discussion in Michaud (1998) on the Theil procedure.

particular, the levels of reliability associated with the forecasts provide a great deal of control of the results, from reflecting largely the historic return estimates to largely the return forecasts. The analyst soon comes to appreciate the interaction of reliability level and historic relationships for designing the optimization inputs and obtaining maximum benefit from the forecasts consistent with beliefs.

## Benefits

The reader may find the asset allocation mixed estimation results in Table 11.1 fairly obvious and largely anticipatable. However, such a procedure is often a world away from the ad hoc return procedures and MV asset allocations prevalent in the investment community. The results in Exhibit 11.1 do not differ drastically from the historic data efficient frontier in spite of the forecasts. This is often not the case with ad hoc returns in practice. Many procedures for developing return forecasts do not consider historic data in a mixed estimation framework and often lead to dramatically different and unstable optimized portfolios. Mixed estimation is likely to have a first-order impact on the stability and investment benefit of MV optimization asset allocation.

*A cautionary note:* Although the mixed estimation process is very flexible, it is also prone to user error. Successful implementation often requires experience and patience with the procedure as well as significant attention to detail.

## Equity Return Forecasts and Mixed Estimation

Theil-Goldberger mixed estimation may be very useful in enhancing return forecasts used in equity portfolio optimization.[4] Many equity return forecasts are based on historic factor-return linear regressions. Managers often have exogenous information that is largely independent of historic data that may be useful in forecasting stock return. Examples of exogenous information may include changes in monetary and fiscal policy, market structure, and political events not well reflected in historic data. Theil-Goldberger mixed estimation provides a convenient and rigorous framework for the integration of exogenous information into linear regression forecasts of stock return.

---

[4] There are many issues on appropriate methods for developing return forecasts. These issues involve a very wide range of active management techniques and are beyond the scope of this text. Michaud (1998) provides a recent review of a number of return forecasting issues for institutional global equity portfolio management and an example of the use of Theil-Goldberger mixed estimation in forecasting returns.

**Exhibit 11.1:** Index-Relative and Mixed Estimate Efficient Frontiers

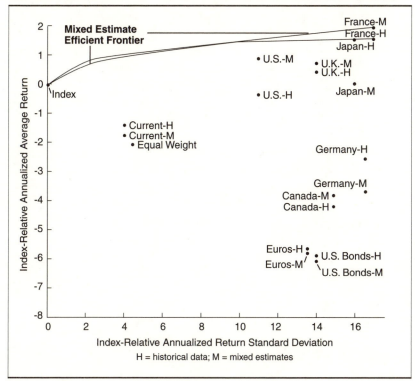

*Note:* H = historical data; M = mixed estimates

Few active equity managers use Theil-Goldberger methods for forecasting active returns. However, such methods are often a natural extension of many institutional stock valuation frameworks and internal procedures. For many equity managers, this largely unexplored technology has the potential of adding much value to asset management. Forecast returns that are consistent with asset variability and factor interrelationships are more likely to lead to optimized portfolios with investment value.

*Chapter* **12**

# Avoiding Optimization Errors

$O$ptimizers are useful for assigning airport gates and routing telephone calls, as well as for optimizing portfolios. Therefore, it should not be surprising that an optimizer requires a great deal of information specific to the investment process if it is going to find investment-relevant portfolios. The operating principle for defining an optimization is that more information is better than less as long as it is reliable. Several procedures, developed largely from institutional experience, are useful for enhancing the investment value of an optimization. Most apply to equity portfolio optimization.

## Scaling Inputs

Improperly scaled inputs are perhaps the single most serious source of errors made in formulating an optimization. In an equity portfolio optimization, there are three basic classes of security inputs: expected returns, trading costs, and risk estimates. In the many cases when the input units are not comparable, optimization results are unlikely to have investment value.

Institutional forecasts of stock returns are generally relative valuations or rankings of stock values.[1] Relative valuations need scaling to be useful as inputs to most optimizers. The appropriate scaling transforms the return forecast into the "return on average associated with the forecast." Proper scaling of return forecasts allows comparability with trading costs, risk estimates, and other inputs in the optimization.[2]

---

[1] Forecasts of expected returns might be relative valuations even when they resemble actual returns. For example, Michaud and Davis (1982) show that dividend discount model returns may only have ordinal or stock ranking information.

[2] Ambachtsheer (1977) pioneered the development of the scaling formula for forecast

**133**

The scaling formula is the product of two quantities:

1. the assumed level of information or correlation between the forecast and ex post return and

2. the expected volatility or standard deviation of ex post returns.

The first quantity is the information correlation or coefficient (IC) of the forecast. The IC and expected volatility may vary by market, sector, industry, and analyst.

The scaling formula for forecast returns has an important subtlety that has often led to error. In many cases, the two components of the scaling formula are inversely related. For example, the IC of a forecast for utility stocks may be higher than for growth stocks, but the level of ex ante volatility may be less. Consequently, the product or scale factor for utility stock forecasts may not differ significantly from that for growth stocks.

Although stock return forecasts are often given in monthly return units, some commercial risk estimate services are provided in weekly units. Inconsistent risk and return units may have a negative impact on the optimization. In some commercial optimizers, the optimized portfolio depends on the values of the parameters of a quadratic "utility" or "risk aversion" function.[3] In this case, the units of the returns and risk estimates affect the solution. However, many portfolio optimizers now include an option that allows the user to ignore risk model units.[4]

The manager must also properly scale expected returns relative to trading cost estimates.[5] Trading costs generally vary by market, hold-

---

returns. Michaud (1989a; appendix, 40–41) generalized the scaling process and developed some of its properties using a linear regression framework. In some cases, a more general regression framework may be appropriate.

[3] An optimizer may define a single optimal portfolio on the efficient frontier based on preset values of quadratic "utility function" parameters that define the relative importance of portfolio risk and expected return. One problem is that the choice of default values of the utility parameters may not be appropriate for a given investor. Another problem is that the parameters may have little intuitive investment meaning. In addition, the default values may obscure limitations of the optimizer or risk model. For example, default parameters may be set to choose efficient portfolios near the top of the efficient frontier. The optimizer, in this case, may do little more than find large expected return portfolios. Often, a more meaningful objective is to define an optimal portfolio in terms of the desired level of risk. For optimizers defined by utility function parameters, the manager can compute efficient portfolios with desired risk levels by varying parameter values.

[4] By allowing the specification of portfolio residual risk directly, a properly formulated stock portfolio optimizer operates independently of the scaling of risk estimates relative to the return inputs and trading costs.

[5] The three components of total trading costs are fees (including taxes), market impact, and opportunity. The careful estimation of all three components of trading costs is a critical element in the likely investment success of a portfolio optimization.

ing period, investment style, and asset class. For example, a value strategy may have a much lower portfolio turnover rate than a growth stock strategy. In this case, the average turnover rate may affect the relative scaling of return forecasts to trading costs.

Although the effort may be significant, proper scaling of all optimization inputs is essential. Poorly scaled optimizations usually generate investment-irrelevant optimized portfolios.

## Financial Reality

It seems obvious to insist that optimization inputs are consistent with financial reality. Yet, in many cases, optimization inputs do not make investment sense.

A surprisingly common error concerns active return forecasts. By definition, the index-weighted sum of active returns must equal zero. In investment terms, an index can never beat itself. Yet, institutional active returns often do not satisfy this necessary condition. Consequently, the optimization may have little investment value. Note that the index-weighted sum constraint is often useful for conditioning historic regressions for forecasting returns.

## Liquidity Factors

For a large trust department or mutual fund portfolio, or for a small-capitalization stock portfolio, the capital value of the fund may be significant in terms of the percentage of a security's outstanding market value. For example, a 1% change in a holding may represent a large amount of capital relative to the size of the firm. Such considerations are related to trading cost, where the trading cost function depends on portfolio size and is nonlinear. This is an example of the inherent position-dependent character of portfolio optimization.

A related issue is liquidity and capitalization in asset allocation. Country equity and fixed income markets may differ significantly in size and liquidity. A mean variance (MV) asset allocation that does not consider relative liquidity and size may lead to irrelevant portfolios. Some methods for considering such factors include nonlinear trading cost constraints and benchmark optimization.

## Constraints

Institutional portfolio optimizations often include many kinds of constraints. Sector and industry membership constraints are a simple way to control portfolio risk. Constraints may reflect investment strategy or market outlook information that is exogenous to return forecasts. Constraints may be useful for imposing quality controls on the portfolio management process. Constraints are also useful for controlling portfolio structure and avoiding inadvertent risk exposures. When no information is available, it is often appropriate to keep factor and group exposures close to index weights. The downside of portfolio constraints is that they can lead to significant opportunity costs on investment performance if not properly used. Overconstrained portfolios may be substantially riskier than they appear.[6]

The large number of constraints in many institutional portfolio optimizations have evolved from valuable, hard-earned investment experience. Investment practice may often reflect the historic need to overcome the many limitations of current MV portfolio optimizers and risk models. However, an informed statistical view of portfolio optimization may reduce the need for many constraints and the opportunity costs and risks associated with overconstrained portfolios.

## Biased Portfolio Characteristics

As a general principle, any optimized portfolio characteristic is biased because estimation error accumulates in the optimization objective function. One important example is that the risk of an optimized portfolio is a downward-biased estimate of its true value. This means that the out-of-sample risk of an optimized portfolio is likely to be larger than that estimated by the risk model and the optimization. One method of evaluating the unbiased risk of an optimized portfolio is to subscribe to two competent risk measurement services. The recommended procedure is to optimize the portfolio with one risk model and evaluate portfolio risk with the other. Although it is not foolproof, the two-risk measurement method can help to realistically estimate out-of-sample portfolio risk.

The same bias is present for any other optimized portfolio characteristic. For example, a manager may want to maximize dividend yield or minimize portfolio beta. A maximized dividend yield or minimized beta portfolio is likely to have a much smaller dividend yield or larger beta out-of-sample than that estimated in the optimization.

---

[6] An overly risk-constrained or factor-constrained portfolio may have much more out of-sample risk than a less constrained portfolio.

Optimizing more than one variable may create additional biases. For example, beta and dividend yield have a negative correlation. Optimizing correlated variables in the same optimization can create synergistic biases and unpredictable portfolio behavior.

In general, the more demands placed on the optimization, the more likely the out-of-sample performance of the optimized portfolio will disappoint. Such effects are endemic to all optimization processes. To be effective, a user should be aware of an optimizer's inherent limitations in using statistically estimated data and conservative in demands made of the optimization process.

## Index Funds and Optimizers

The purpose of an index fund is to track an index. One method for constructing index funds is to use MV optimization. The objective is to minimize the residual or tracking error. Because there are no return estimates, an index fund optimization is significantly more stable than a more typical MV optimization. For this reason, optimization may appear as the tool of choice for constructing index-tracking portfolios. However, because of competitive pressures, manager tolerance for tracking error is generally much smaller than for active portfolios. Even small errors in tracking error estimation can have (and have had) significant negative business consequences.

There are two alternative ways to construct index funds in practice: replication and stratified sampling. *Index replication* is constructing an index-weighted portfolio consisting of all the securities in the index.[7] *Stratification* is a statistical sampling procedure for constructing a representative sample portfolio of securities in the index, usually based on index-weighted representative tiers or sectors of securities in the index. The three procedures differ in comprehensiveness of representation of the index: Replication is most comprehensive, whereas optimization is usually the least.

Various considerations determine which procedure to choose in a given situation. Minimum tracking error and rebalancing issues may make replication the method of choice for long-term investors. In some cases, where the liquidity or holding costs of stocks in an index is a major consideration, optimization or stratified sampling may be more appropriate alternatives. In some emerging markets, where a reliable risk model may not be available, stratification may be the procedure of choice.

---

[7] In practice, the portfolio may exclude many small stocks.

## Optimization from Cash

The appropriate procedure for optimizing an equity portfolio may depend on whether the optimization starts from cash or from a fully invested equity portfolio (Erlich 1997). To frame the issue, note that any equity portfolio is decomposable into two portfolios: an index fund and a pure active or arbitrage portfolio.[8] If we suppose an indefinite holding period for the invested assets, rebalancing may occur many times over the life of the fund.

An active manager optimizes the portfolio according to the active return forecasts. Conceptually, the index is the appropriate starting portfolio. When optimizing from cash, however, the objective of optimally investing in the active or arbitrage portfolio conflicts with the need to convert cash into the index. The active return forecasts are relevant for a single, often relatively short-term, forecast period. Each rebalancing period has different active return forecasts. In contrast, the index component of the fund is relatively stable. Eventually, the cost of converting cash into the stock index is paid. The optimizer has to compromise between the dual objectives of finding an optimal arbitrage portfolio and investing in the stock index portfolio. Rebalancing periods when the purchase of the index fund is incomplete exposes the optimized portfolio to unnecessary and irrelevant risk and trading costs.

A preferable procedure is to invest cash in two optimization steps. First, find an optimal portfolio from cash, omitting active return forecasts, that considers the investor's objectives and constraints, including residual risk target, desired number of securities, and trading cost estimates. This step defines a neutral or index-like portfolio that reflects the normal constraints and objectives that are part of the relatively stable structure of the fund. The second step starts with the neutral portfolio to define an optimal active portfolio as a function of the active return forecasts. The arbitrage component of the active portfolio in the second-step optimization reflects tradeoffs between return forecasts, risk, and trading costs, independent of the need to convert cash into equities. Because the cost of buying the neutral portfolio has to be paid, there is no overall increase in trading cost over the normal life of the fund.

The Erlich two-step optimization procedure balances the long-term objective of buying the neutral portfolio with the shorter-term objective

---

[8] The weights of the arbitrage portfolio sum to zero while the index fund weights sum to one. See Michaud (1993) for further discussion.

of implementing the active return forecasts. The procedure is likely to result in better performance, less risk, more stability during early rebalancings, and a reduction in overall trading costs.

Cash optimization may also be useful when adding cash to an equity portfolio. More generally, two-step optimization may be useful when there is a change in the benchmark portfolio or in other long-term characteristics of the fund. The importance of two-step optimization may increase as the size of the stock universe and level of active portfolio risk increases. For low-risk and single-country equity portfolios, the benefits may not be significant.

## Forecast Return Limitations

Useful optimized portfolios require careful control of portfolio structure. This is because forecast returns may have implicit structural biases that are not part of the information in the stock valuation process.

Generally, active equity optimization returns are adjusted for systematic risk. However, there are many open theoretical and practical issues with estimating the return associated with systematic risk. For example, Kandel and Stambaugh (1995) note some important limitations of widely used econometric estimation methods. From another perspective, Berk's (1995) theoretical analysis suggests that many systematic risk frameworks may not correctly reflect the risk of small stocks. In addition, the proper theoretical framework for estimating systematic risk remains controversial in some cases.[9]

Another source of biases may come from the structure of the returns. Suppose that the stock forecasts are market sector neutral.[10] For example, a forecast may be based on a factor-return regression that includes sector dummy variables to adjust for sector returns. Nevertheless, the unconstrained optimized portfolio may exhibit large overweights and underweights in various market sectors. If there is no sector information in the return forecast, why are there sector underweights and overweights?

Variables used to forecast return, such as the book-to-price ratio, are likely to have larger than average values in some sectors than in others. A larger than average value of the forecast factors in a sector is likely to lead to a larger than average value of forecast return in the sec-

---

[9] For example, Shanken (1992, 1995) provides critiques of the arbitrage pricing theory framework that is the basis of many commercial models of equity risk measurement.

[10] Michaud (1998) provides an example.

tor. Consequently, all other things being the same, the unconstrained optimized portfolio is overweighted in some sectors and underweighted in others. However, by definition of a sector neutral forecast, there is no sector weighting information in the return.[11] In this case, the structure of returns leads to inadvertent portfolio biases that are not consistent with the sources of information in the forecast. One simple way to eliminate inadvertent biases in optimized portfolios is to impose index weight constraints on factor exposures that do not reflect forecast return information.

Biases in forecast returns may be pervasive and are often very subtle. Analysts and investment managers must be diligent in detecting and eliminating such biases. Portfolio optimization is likely to fail to provide useful investment portfolios unless the process is well formulated and consistent with risk estimation and the relevant sources of information in the forecasts.

## Conclusion

Avoiding implementation errors is important for capturing and enhancing the investment value of optimizers. Thoughtful consideration of investment theory and intuition, investor objectives, forecast return biases, and optimizer behavior leads to specialized techniques that may have a significant positive impact on optimized portfolio performance.

---

[11] It should be noted that other formulations of forecast return may have sector-weighting information. The point of the example is to show that inadvertent portfolio bets may appear in an unconstrained optimized portfolio.

# Epilogue

*T*he most serious limitations of mean-variance (MV) efficiency as a practical tool of investment management are instability and ambiguity. Small input errors lead to large errors in the optimized portfolio. By maximizing the use of statistical errors in parameter estimates, an MV optimized portfolio may often have little, if any, investment value. In addition, because of instability, MV efficiency may be ambiguous and poorly defined in practice.

The practical limitations of MV optimization are not a reflection of conceptual flaws in Markowitz MV efficiency but of implementation. MV optimization overfits statistically estimated data. The power of the algorithm is generally far greater than the level of investment information in the inputs. Most proposed alternatives to MV efficiency also have significant practical limitations, and typically do not improve instability or ambiguity.

Implementation errors often reflect a lack of understanding of the fundamental statistical nature of MV efficiency. MV optimization is essentially a statistical procedure similar in important respects to constrained multivariate linear regression. Statistical procedures require statistical analysis. Although statistical methods have developed naturally in the context of multivariate linear regression, the history of MV efficiency has had a limiting effect on its statistical development. Statistically based techniques, such as the resampled efficient frontier and region, statistical portfolio analysis, mixed estimation, Stein estimation, and benchmark optimization, help to improve the investment value of an MV optimized portfolio. In addition, investment theory and institutional practices that have evolved from experience and the character of investment information play important roles in improving practical application. Although each procedure may add value to MV optimization, together they offer the potential of substantial improvements in investment performance.

Historically, large segments of the institutional investment management community have ignored MV optimization. In hindsight, the reason is simply because MV optimization did not work or did not work well enough to add investment value in its original formulation. Yet the investment community has much at stake in a better understanding of MV efficiency and portfolio optimization. MV optimization properly used is potentially the universal engine of institutional asset management.

Much effort remains to improve the investment value of MV optimization. There are many open issues. In particular, Stein estimators, economic liability models, portfolio statistical analysis methods, and more efficient computational algorithms have much potential for improving the current state of the art. An awareness of their importance will, it is hoped, spur funding and research in these areas. However, the fact that the limitations of MV optimization have been ignored for so long, particularly when many of the techniques for enhancing investment value have been available for many years, raises troubling issues of the state of sophistication of institutional research and investment practice and of academic-practitioner relationships. Perhaps some lasting lessons can be learned for the future.

# Bibliography

Alexander, Gordon, and Jack Clark Francis. 1986. *Portfolio Analysis,* 3d ed. Englewood Cliffs, NJ: Prentice-Hall.

Ambachtsheer, Keith. 1977. "Where are the Customers' Alphas?" *Journal of Portfolio Management* 4(1):52–56.

Barry, C.B. 1974. "Portfolio Analysis Under Uncertain Means." *Journal of Finance* 29(2):515–522.

Bawa, Vijay, Stephen Brown, and Roger Klein. 1979. *Estimation Risk and Optimal Portfolio Choice.* Amsterdam: North Holland.

Beale, E.M.L. 1955. "On Minimizing a Convex Function Subject to Linear Inequalities." *Journal of the Royal Statistical Society* (B)17:173–184.

———. 1959. "On Quadratic Programming." *Naval Research Logistics Quarterly* 6(3):227–243.

Berk, Jonathan B. 1995. "A Critique of Size Related Anomalies." *Review of Financial Studies* 8(2):275–286.

Black, Fischer. 1972. "Capital Market Equilibrium with Restricted Borrowing." *Journal of Business* 45(3):444–455.

———. 1989. "Universal Hedging: How to Optimize Currency Risk and Reward in International Equity Portfolios." *Financial Analysts Journal* 45(4):16–22.

——— and Myron Scholes. 1973. "The Pricing of Options and Corporate Liabilities." *Journal of Political Economy* 81(3):637–654.

——— and Robert Litterman. 1992. "Global Portfolio Optimization." *Financial Analysts Journal* 48(5)28–43.

Brinson, Gary, L. Randolph Hood, and Gil Beebower. 1986. "Determinants of Portfolio Performance." *Financial Analysts Journal* 42(4)39–44.

Brown, Stephen. 1976. "Optimal Portfolio Choice under Uncertainty." Unpublished Ph.D. dissertation, University of Chicago.

Chopra, Vijay. 1991. "Mean-Variance Revisited: Near-Optimal Portfolios and Sensitivity to Input Variations." *Russell Research Commentary* (December).

Copas, J.B. 1983. "Regression Prediction and Shrinkage." *Journal of the Royal Statistical Society* (B) 45:311–354.

Dey, D.K., and C. Srinivasan. 1985. "Estimation of a Covariance Matrix Under Stein's Loss." *Annals of Statistics* 13(4):1581–1591.

Efron, B., and C. Morris. 1973. "Stein's Estimation Rule and Its Competitors—An Empirical Bayes Approach." *Journal of the American Statistical Association* 68(341):117–130.

_____. 1975. "Data Analysis Using Stein's Estimator and its Generalizations." *Journal of the American Statistical Association* 70(350):311–319.

_____. 1977. "Stein's Paradox in Statistics." *Scientific American* 236 (May 1977):119–127.

_____ and Robert Tibshirani. 1993. *An Introduction to the Bootstrap.* New York: Chapman and Hall.

Erlich, Paul. 1997. "Cash Optimization." Acadian Research, Boston, Mass. Memo.

Fama, Eugene, and James MacBeth. 1973. "Risk, Return and Equilibrium—Empirical Tests." *Journal of Political Economy* 81(3):607–636.

_____ and Kenneth French. 1992. "The Cross-Section of Expected Stock Returns." *Journal of Finance* 47(2)427–465.

Farrell, James L., Jr. 1983. *Guide to Portfolio Management.* New York: McGraw-Hill, 168–174.

Fisher, Lawrence. 1975. "Using Modern Portfolio Theory to Maintain an Efficiently Diversified Portfolio." *Financial Analysts Journal* 31(N):73–85.

Frank, M. and P. Wolfe. 1956. "An Algorithm for Quadratic Programming." *Naval Research Logistics Quarterly* 3:95–110.

Frost, P. and J. Savarino. 1986. "An Empirical Bayes Approach to Efficient Portfolio Selection." *Journal of Financial and Quantitative Analysis* 21(3):293–305.

_____. 1988. "For Better Performance: Constrain Portfolio Weights." *Journal of Portfolio Management* 15(1):29–34.

Geweke, John. 1986."Exact Inference in the Inequality Constrained Normal Linear Regression Model." *Journal of Applied Econometrics* (1):127–141.

Hakansson, Nils. 1971a. "Capital Growth and the Mean-Variance Approach to Portfolio Selection." *Journal of Financial and Quantitative Analysis* 6(1): 517–557.

_____. 1971b. "Multi-Period Mean-Variance Analysis: Towards a General Theory of Portfolio Choice." *Journal of Finance* 26(4):857–884.

Hensel, Chris D., Don Ezra, and John Ilkiw. 1991. "The Importance of the Asset Allocation Decision." *Financial Analyst Journal* 47(4):65–72.

James, W., and C. Stein. 1961. "Estimation with Quadratic Loss." *Proceedings of the Fourth Berkeley Symposium on Probability and Statistics* Berkeley: University of California Press, 361–379.

Jobson, J.D. 1991. "Confidence Regions for the Mean-Variance Efficient Set: An Alternative Approach to Estimation Risk." *Review of Quantitative Finance and Accounting* 1:235–257.

_____ and Bob Korkie. 1981. "Putting Markowitz Theory to Work." *Journal of Portfolio Management* 7(4):70–74.

_____. 1981. "Estimation for Markowitz Efficient Portfolios." *Journal of the American Statistical Association* 75(371):544–554..

_____. 1982. "Potential Performance and Tests of Portfolio Efficiency." *Journal of Financial Economics* 10(4):433–466.

_____. 1985. "Some Tests of Linear Asset Pricing with Multivariate Normality." *Canadian Journal of Administrative Sciences* 2(1):114–138.

_____. 1985. "Statistical Inference in Two Parameter Portfolio Theory with Multiple Regression Software." *Journal of Financial and Quantitative Analysis* 18(2):189–197.

_____ and Vinod Ratti. 1979. "Improved Estimation for Markowitz Efficient Portfolios Using James-Stein Type Estimators." In *Proceedings of the Business and Economics Statistics Section* in Washington D.C., August 13–16, by the American Statistical Association, 279–284.

_____. 1980. "Improved Estimation and Selection Rules for Markowitz Portfolios." *Proceedings of the Annual Meeting of the Western Finance Association* (As above.)

Johnson, Richard, and Dean Wichern. 1992. *Applied Multivariate Statistical Analysis*. 3d ed. Saddle River, NJ: Prentice-Hall.

Jorion, Philippe. 1986. "Bayes-Stein Estimation for Portfolio Analysis." *Journal of Financial and Quantitative Analysis* 21(3):279–292.

_____. 1992. "Portfolio Optimization in Practice." *Financial Analysts Journal* 48(1)68–74.

Judge, George, R. Carter Hill, William Griffiths, Helmut Lutkepohl, and Tsoung-Chao Lee. 1988. *Introduction to the Theory and Practice of Econometrics*, 2d ed., New York: Wiley.

Kandel, Shmuel, and Robert Stambaugh. 1995. "Portfolio Inefficiency and the Cross-section of Expected Returns." *Journal of Finance* 50(1):157–184.

Kroll, Yoram, Haim Levy, and Harry Markowitz. 1984. "Mean-Variance Versus Direct Utility Maximization." *Journal of Finance* 39(1):47–61.

Ledoit, Olivier. 1994. "Portfolio Selection: Improved Covariance Matrix Estimation," Sloan School of Management, Working paper (November).

_____. 1997. "Improved Estimation of the Covariance Matrix of Stock Returns with an Application to Portfolio Selection." Anderson Graduate School of Management at UCLA, Working paper (March).

Levy, Haim, and Harry Markowitz. 1979. "Approximating Expected Utility by a Function of the Mean and Variance." *American Economic Review* 69(3):308–317.

Liebowitz, Martin. 1986. "The Dedicated Bond Portfolio in Pension Funds, Part I: Motivations and Basics; Part II; Immunization, Horizon Matching and Contingent Procedures." *Financial Analysts Journal* 42(1):69–75; 42(2):47–57.

Lintner, John. 1965. "The Valuation of Risk Assets and the Selection of Risky Investments in Stock Portfolios and Capital Budgets." *Review of Economics and Statistics* 47(1):13–37.

Markowitz, Harry. 1956. "The Optimization of a Quadratic Function Subject to Linear Constraints." *Naval Research Logistics Quarterly* 3(1/2):111–133.

_____. 1991. *Portfolio Selection: Efficient Diversification of Investments.* New York: Wiley, 1959; 2d ed., Cambridge, MA: Basil Blackwell.

_____. 1976. "Investment for the Long-Run: New Evidence for an Old Rule." *Journal of Finance* 31(5):1273–1286.

_____. 1987. *Mean-Variance Analysis in Portfolio Choice and Capital Markets.* Cambridge, MA: Blackwell.

Merton, Robert C. 1973. "The Theory of Rational Option Pricing." *Bell Journal of Economics* 4(1):141–183.

Michaud, Richard. 1976. "Pension Fund Investment Policy." Presented to the Institute for Quantitative Research in Finance, Spring Seminar.

_____. 1981. "Risk Policy and Long-Term Investment." *Journal of Financial and Quantitative Analysis* 16(2):147–167.

_____. 1989a. "The Markowitz Optimization Enigma: Is Optimized Optimal?" *Financial Analysts Journal* 45(1):31–42.

_____. 1989b. "Economic Surplus and Pension Asset Management." *Merrill Lynch Pension Executive Review* 2(1):7–13.

_____. 1989c. "Pension Policy and Benchmark Optimization." *Investment Management Review* 3(8):25–30.

_____. 1993. "Are Long-Short Equity Strategies Superior?" *Financial Analysts Journal* 49(6):44–49.

_____. 1998. *Market Anomalies, Investment Styles and Global Stock Selection.* Charlottesville, VA: The Research Foundation of the Institute of Chartered Financial Analyst. Forthcoming.

_____ and James Monahan. 1981. "Comparisons of Optimal versus Stationary Investment Policies over Time." Presented to the Institute for Quantitative Research in Finance, Spring Seminar.

_____ and Paul Davis. 1982. "Valuation Model Bias and the Scale Structure of Dividend Discount Returns." *Journal of Finance* 37(2):563–573.

Perold, Andre. 1984. "Large Scale Portfolio Optimization." *Management Science* 30(10):1143–1160.

Roll, Richard. 1977. "A Critique of the Asset Pricing Theory's Tests, Part I: On Past and Potential Testability of the Theory." *Journal of Financial Economics* 4(2):129–176.

_____. 1979. "Testing a Portfolio of Ex Ante Mean-Variance Efficiency." *TIMS Studies in the Management Studies* 11:135–149.

———. 1992. "A Mean/Variance Analysis of Tracking Error." *Journal of Portfolio Management* 18(4):13–22.

——— and Stephen Ross. 1994. "On the Cross-Sectional Relation Between Expected Returns and Betas." *Journal of Finance* 49(1):101–121.

Rosenberg, Barr. 1974. "Extra-Market Component of Covariance in Security Returns." *Journal of Financial and Qualitative Analysis* March 9(2):263–273.

Rosenberg, Barr, and Walt McKibben. 1973. "The Prediction of Systematic and Specific Risk in Common Stocks." *Journal of Financial and Quantitative Analysis* 8(3):317–333.

——— and James Guy. 1973. "Beta Investment Fundamentals." *Financial Analysis Journal* 32(3):60–72; 32(4):62–70.

Ross, Stephen. 1975. "Return, Risk and Arbitrage." In *Studies in Risk and Return*, edited by I. Friend and J. Bicksler. Cambridge, MA: Ballinger.

———. 1976. "The Arbitrage Theory of Capital Asset Pricing." *Journal of Economic Theory* 13(3):341–360.

Rubinstein, Mark. 1973. "A Comparative Statics Analysis of Risk Premiums." *Journal of Business* 46(4):605–615.

Shanken, Jay. 1985. "Multivariate Tests of the Zero-Beta CAPM. *Journal of Financial Economics* 14(3):327–357.

———. 1992. "The Current State of the Arbitrage Pricing Theory." *Journal of Finance* 47(4):1569–1574.

———. 1996. "Statistical Methods in Tests of Portfolio Efficiency: A Synthesis." In *Handbook of Statistics*, vol. 14, edited by G.S. Maddala and C.R. Rao. Amsterdam: Elsevier.

Sharpe, William. 1963. "A Simplified Model for Portfolio Analysis." *Management Science* 9(2):277–293.

———. 1964. "Capital Asset Prices: A Theory of Market Equilibrium Under Conditions of Risk." *Journal of Finance* 19(3):425–442.

———. 1970. *Portfolio Theory and Capital Markets*. New York: McGraw-Hill.

———. 1974. "Imputing Expected Security Returns from Portfolio Composition." *Journal of Financial and Quantitative Analysis* 9(3):463–472.

———. 1985. *Investments*. Englewood Cliffs, NJ: Prentice-Hall, 666–670.

Stein, Charles. 1955. "Inadmissibility of the Usual Estimator of the Mean of a Multivariate Normal Distribution." *Proceedings of the Third Berkeley Symposium on Probability and Statistics.* Berkeley: University of California Press.

Stein, Charles. 1982. Series of lectures given at the University of Washington, Seattle.

Theil, Henri. 1971. *Principles of Econometrics*, New York: Wiley, 282–293.

——— and A.S. Goldberger. 1961. "On Pure and Mixed Statistical Estimation in Economics." *International Economic Review* 2(1):65–78.

Wolfe, P. 1959. "The Simplex Algorithm for Quadratic Programming." *Econometrica* 27(3):382–398.

Young, William, and Robert Trent. 1969. "Geometric Mean Approximations of Individual Security and Portfolio Performance." *Journal of Financial and Quantitative Analysis* 4(2):179–199.

# Index

Numbers followed by the letter e
refer to exhibits; numbers followed
by the letter n refer to notes; numbers
followed by the letter t refer to tables.

Acceptance levels, analysis of, 43–45,
    44e
Accrued benefit obligation (ABO),
    119
Ambiguity, xiv, 3–4, 34–35, 141
    and portfolio efficiency, 77–79
Arbitrage pricing theory (APT), 12
Asset allocation, 11–12
    ad hoc inputs and, 127–129
    through benchmark optimization,
        101–113
    example of, 13–15, 14t
    long-term, 29n
Asset-liability simulation, 3
Asset-liability studies, 29–31
    limitations of, 30–31
Asset management
    enhancement of, xv, 141, 142
    facets of, xiii
    long-term, 3
    MV optimization and, 2–3
Asset pricing models, tests of, 41–42

Bayesian procedures, 84–85
Benchmark optimization, 101
    benchmark-relative, 102–105
    comparison of types of, 109
    implied-return, 105–108
    and investment policy, 116
Benchmark-relative asset allocation,
    102–105
    benefit of, 105, 113
    for pension fund, 122–126
Book-to-price ratio, 139
Bootstrapping, 34n

Capital asset pricing model (CAPM),
    12, 42

Capitalization weights, 99
Compound return, 27
Confidence intervals, 71
    simultaneous, 75–77
Confidence region testing, 72–79
    for sample mean vector, 80
    for simultaneous intervals, 81
Corner portfolio, 21
Correlation, 7
Covariance, 7n
    defined, 94n
    estimation of, 94–97, 99
Covariance matrix, 7n, 85
    defined, 95n
    estimators of, 97, 98
Critical-line algorithm, 21n

Data resampling, 34n
Diversification, benefits of, xiii

Economic liability model, 116
    and pension investment policy,
        122–126
Economic pension liability models,
    118
Efficient frontier, 1, 2e, 14n, 15e
    index-relative, 102, 103–105, 104e,
        105e
    for index-relative asset allocation,
        131e
    for mixed estimate forecast, 131e
    resampled, 55, 61, 72–75, 103–104,
        105e
    residual risk-return, 10, 11e
    return premium, 18e
    scaled, 108, 110e
    variance of, 36–39, 38e
Efficient frontier portfolios, analysis
    of, 50–54
Endowment fund, investment policy
    for, 117
Equal correlations, 99
Equilibrium, 111

Equity markets, return data of, 13n
Equity portfolio optimization, 12–13
Equity return forecasts, 130–131
Erlich two-stage optimization, 138–139
Estimation errors, 36, 56
    effect of, 3
    minimizing, 4–5
Expected return, 7

Forecasts. *See* Return forecasts
Frost-Savarino estimator, 93–94

Generalized least squares (GLS)
    regression, 97
Geometric mean, 27–28

Hakansson efficiency, 28n

Identity matrix, 99
Implied-return asset allocation, 105–108
    advantages of, 108
    compared with benchmark-relative
        active asset allocation, 109
    implications of, 107–108, 107e
    and return forecasting, 112
    scaled, 109–112
Index funds, 13n, 137
Index-relative active asset allocation,
        102n
    efficient frontier of, 131e
    mixed estimates and, 128–130
    of pension plans, 117–126
    Roll's analysis of, 112–113
Information coefficient (IC), 135
Input estimation
    admissible estimators for, 84
    importance of, 83
Inputs
    estimation of, 83, 84
    mixed estimation, 128
    optimization, 56
    scaling of, 133–135
Investment policy, 115
    economic liability and, 122–126
    MV efficiency framework to
        define, 116

James-Stein estimator, 85–86
    characteristics of, 86–90
    testing resampled and MV
        efficiency, 90–93
    uses of, 97
Jobson, J.D., 33–36

K index models, 99
Korkie, Bob, 33–36

Lambda-associated resampled
        efficient portfolios, 66–69
Ledoit estimator, 96–97
    use of, 97, 99
Liabilities
    actuarial estimations of, 118–120
    economic, 116
    of pension plan, 119–120
    variable, 120–122
Linear programming, 31–32
Long-term asset allocation, 29n
Long-term objectives, MV efficiency
        and, 27

Market portfolio, defining, 111
Markowitz efficient frontier. *See*
        Efficient frontier
Markowitz mean-variance (MV)
        efficiency. *See* MV efficiency
MATLAB language, xvi
Mean, 8, 8e
    estimation of, 85–94
Mean absolute deviation, 23
Mean-variance (MV) efficiency. *See*
        MV efficiency
Minimax, defined, 96n
Mixed estimation forecasts, 128–130
    benefits of, 130
    efficient frontier for, 131e
    and equity return forecasts, 130–133
    and index-relative active asset
        allocation, 128–130
    inputs for, 128
Monte Carlo simulations, 29–31
    example of, 34n
Multiperiod analyses, 26–29
MV efficiency, 1–2, 2e
    barriers to acceptance of, xiv

calculation of, 10–11, 20
defined, 9
James-Stein test of, 90–93
limitations of, xiv, 3–4, 34–35, 77, 141
misuse of, 115–116
multiperiod analysis of, 28
objections to, xiv, 3, 77
parametric quadratic programming and, 21–22
portfolios generated under, 60
statistical character of, 36
MV optimization
advantages of, 26
alternatives to, 23–32
application of, 2–3, 11–13
benchmark, 101–113
constraints on, 9–10
enhancements to, 141, 142
estimation error and, 3, 36, 56
exact vs. approximate, 22
Frost-Savarino, 93–94
implementation errors and, 141
of index funds, 137
inputs for, 17t, 19t
investment policy based on, 115
of multiple variables, 137
practicality of, 39–40
resolving limitations of, 4–5
return forecasts and, 127
skepticism toward, 141–142
Stein estimators and, 85

Nonvariance risk measures, 23–25

Optimization
according to active return forecasts, 138
bias and, 139
from cash, 138–139
Erlich, 138–139
Optimization inputs, true and estimated, 56
Optimizers
commercial, 134
pitfalls of using, 134n
utility of, 133
Options, 24

Parametric quadratic programming, 20–21
Pension plans
benchmark optimization of, 117, 122–126
benefit obligations of, 119–120
liabilities of, 119–120
plan termination obligations, 118–119
termination consequences, 120–121
Pivot point, 21
Portfolio optimization, 12–13
input estimation and, 83, 83n
Portfolio review, 41
acceptance levels and, 42–45
Portfolio statistical analysis, 49
efficient, 50–54
Portfolios
constraints on, 136
corner, 21
efficiency of, xiii
efficiency of, ambiguity of, 77–79
long and short market-neutral equity, xvin
management of, xv
MV efficient, 60
ranking of statistically equivalent, 45–47, 46e
reference, 17t, 18e
resampled efficiency for, 61, 63–66
return distribution of, 24
risk and return of, 7–9, 8e
variables affecting efficiency of, 72

Quadratic programming, 10–11
parametric, 21–22

Rank-associated efficient portfolios, 45–47, 46e
Reference portfolio, 17t, 18e
Relative valuations, scaling of, 133
Replication, index, 137
Resampled efficiency, 56–57
caveats regarding, 61–63
characteristics of, 60–61
and distance functions, 72
James-Stein test of, 90–93
lambda-associated, 66–69

for sign-constrained portfolios, 63–66

tests of, 63–69

virtues of, 57, 58t, 59–60, 59e

Resampled efficient frontier, 55, 55e, 61, 72

confidence regions, 73–75, 74e

Resampling, 34n

Residual return, 10, 11e

Residual risk-return efficient frontier, 10, 11e

Return

expected, 7

implied-return framework and forecasting of, 112

residual, 10, 11e

Return forecasts, 127

bias in, 139

mixed estimation, 128–131

and MV optimization problems, 127–128

scaling and, 133–135

variables for, 139–140

Return premium, 16, 17e, 19t

Reward-risk ratios, 57, 58t, 59

Riemann integral, 43

Risk

commercial estimators of, 134, 136

estimation of, 112

managing, xiii

measures of, 23–25

residual, 10, 11e

Risk aversion, 134

Roll framework, 102n

Sample mean vector, 72

confidence region for, 80

Scaling, and implied returns, 108, 109–112, 110e

Semistandard deviation of return, 23, 24e

Semivariance, 23, 24e

Sharpe ratio, calculation of, 35n

Sharpe-Lintner capital asset pricing model, 1

Sharpe's single-index model, 98, 99

Short selling, and MV optimization, xvi

Simplex algorithm, 21n

Simultaneous confidence intervals, 75–77, 79

confidence regions and, 81

Single-index model, 98, 99

Standard deviation, 7–8, 8e

Statistical equivalence, 38, 38n, 42

Stein estimators, 83, 84

types of, 85–97

Stein-Dey-Srinivasan estimator, 96–97

Stratified sampling, 137

Summation, 7n

Theil-Goldberger mixed estimation, 128

Trading costs, 134–135

components of, 134n

Universal hedging equilibrium, 111n

Utility functions, 25

and input estimation, 97

specificity of, 26

Utility maximization, 25

limitations of, 25–26

Variable benefit obligation (VBO), 119

risk characteristics of, 121

significance of, 120–121

Variable liabilities, 120–121

economic characteristics of, 121–122

Variance, 7n

of MV efficient frontier, 36–39, 38e

Weighting, 7n, 8

Zero-beta portfolio, 42n